Mussolini's *Afrika Korps:*
The Italian Army in North Africa
1940-1943

ABOVE: A native Meharisti NCO showing the distinct arm rank of a Bulucbasci (Sergeant). The tartan pattern sash he is wearing indicates which squadron he belongs to. It was worn around the waist and across the chest. - Author's Collection.

Mussolini's *Afrika Korps:* The Italian Army in North Africa 1940-1943

by Rex Trye

Axis Europa Books

AXIS EUROPA BOOKS
UNIQUE BOOKS ON THE MILITARY HISTORY OF THE AXIS FORCES, 1939-1945
53-20 207th Street, Bayside, NY 11364
fax orders: 1 (718) 229-1352
Phone Orders: (718) 423-9893
URL- http://www.axiseuropa.com

ISBN 1-891227-14-9

Book presentation & design: Antonio J. Munoz
Edited by Antonio Munoz,
Proof reading: Rex Trye, Jack Greene, & Antonio Munoz
Dust jacket design: Antonio Munoz & Rex Trye
color plates: Malcolm Thomas
b&w line drawings: Vincent Wai & Antonio Munoz

CONTENTS

ABOUT THE WRITING STYLE

The author of this work grew up in and received his education using traditional English; That is, that spoken and written form as practiced in the United Kingdom, New Zealand, Australia, etc. This "traditional" version of the English language is different from what has come to be known as "American" English.

For example, in the United Kingdom the letter "u" many times follows the letter "o" in numerous words (i.e.- "colour," "armoured," etc.), while in the Americanized version, we completely omit the "u." Similarly, we Americans "decided" to reverse a few letters in some words (for example, in England they write "metres," whereas in the US, we write "meters," etc.).

Additionally, some words are not capitalized in the "traditional" version, while in the "American" brand of English, they are (and vice-a-versa). Other, more subtle changes and forms exist in both "versions," but suffice it to say that when this book was prepared, the Publisher felt the need to "Americanize" much of the text. This was not done because we favor (favour?) one version or another, but more so because we felt more "comfortable" working with this style.

- The Publisher

PUBLISHER'S FORWARD

It gives me great pleasure and pride to be able to present the English reading public with this, the second work by author and historian, Rex Trye. In his first book, *"Mussolini's Soldiers,"* Mr. Trye introduced the reader to the Italian soldier and narrated how the Italian citizen was transformed, through the political, social and military apparatus of the day, into an Italian soldier. We learned about the regime that backed him and the arms and equipment, training and guidance that he was given before being thrown into battle.

Mr. Trye's detailed analysis allowed us to see the Italian soldier like he had not been presented before in any book- up close and personal. The work, which came out in 1995, is still a best seller and on the "must buy" list of anyone interested in the Italian Army of World War II.

I am proud to present "Mussolini's Afrika Korps," a work that takes the reader into the wadis and deserts of North Africa and continues the story of the Italian soldier during the Second World War. We are first introduced to Italian colonial Libya and how it was governed and administered. The preceding sections of the book describes in typical Trye detail the Italian and Libyan soldiers that made up Mussolini's African army- his "Afrika Korps" if you will, and its arms and equipment.

The Italian campaign against the British and the subsequent arrival of the Germans completes this work, while the epilogue allows the reader to see what occurred to these men and to Libya after the war. The amount of data that Mr. Trye has collected and the way in which he has presented this study leads me to suspect that once again, the author has written what will become " required reading" on the subject.

- Antonio J. Munoz

ABOVE: Mussolini pins a medal of Valor on the banner of the Italian Colonial Corps during his visit to Libya in 1937. - QEII Army Museum, Waiouru, New Zealand.

Photographic and Textual Acknowledgments -

With the writing and research of this book I embarked on a journey of discovery, along the way I met individuals who helped me with my process of learning and in so doing, contributed to the shape and form of this publication. This experience enriched my life and helped focus my perception of the subject matter. I feel humbled by this generous spirit of co-operation and wish to thank the following individuals and institutions.

Sergio Andrenelli, NZ National Arhives, NZ 21 Battalion Association, Zonderwater Block Association, Ricardo Bonaccio, Adriano Boncompagni, Luigi Bonechi, Johan Botha, Mike Brown, Bundsarchiv, James Burd, Raymond Butler, Wayne Butler, Colin Campbell, Greg Carrubba, Luciano Capellino, Howard Christie, Antonio Cioci, Peter Coleman, Peter Cooke, Alan Culhane, Rudy D'Angelo, Keith Davies, Windsor Davis, The late Clive Deippe, Rocco Amedeo DiProspero, Libro DiZinno, Craig Douglas, Franco Fassio, Franco Festa, Michele Figliola, William Frassanito, SA National Defence force, Leonie Gallagah, Richard Garczynski, Cesare Gardellin, Vetrano Gennaro, Jack Greene, Krystyna Von Hennesberg, SA National Museum of Military History, Doris Ho, David Hunter, Steven Hurst, Andre Kirk, Cecilia Kruger, Alexander Turnball Library, Giorgio Lupi, Adrian Malloch, Alessandro Massignani, Dal McGuirk, Otto Meyer, Antonio (Tony) Munoz, QEII Army Memorial Museum, Aldo Nava, John Nicholson, Public Records Office, Nicola Pignato, Wally Rail, Achille Rastelli, Ray Richards, Vito Romano, Domenico Sansotta, Aldo Sbrissa, Ufficio Storico, Richard Taylor, Ugo Tebaldini, Malcolm Thomas, Krystyna von Henneberg, Franco Verzetti, C. Wan, Dos White, Keith Williams, Angela Young, Jack Greene.

INTRODUCTION

Libya was an Italian colonial possession for thirty two years, during that period the Italian Government (in varying degrees) nurtured and sustained this barren territory in an endeavour to make it prosper, it was eventually to be declared the 19th province of Italy. The Italian conquest of Libya was but the latest in a long line of such occupations of Libya by invaders over the centuries, it was not the first time the Italians had been in Libya. In ancient Rome Libya had been a province of the Empire.

The Italians expended a great deal of blood, sweat and tears, plus a fortune in monetary investment (1.8 Billion lire) in an effort to achieve their much vaunted goals of rebuilding this lost Roman province and restoring it to it's past glories. With the coming of World War II, Mussolini launched this still vulnerable and militarily unprepared colony into the maelstrom of a war that was to see all the efforts of the past three decades turn to dust, this left a somber epitaph for the North African colonisation and military aspirations of Italy.

I hope to give the reader some insights through the text and photographs in this book of what the colonisation of Libya meant to the Italians, and to illustrate through the lens of the camera the military forces and weapons utilised by the Italians in their North African misadventure. Before WWII the Libyan desert surface was largely a featureless, flat expanse of sand, rock and occasional clumps of camel thorn. One important change the war brought to this landscape was the litter of battle field debris and larger wrecks.

These became important points of reference for any soldiers passing by. Many photographed these, merely because they broke the monotony of the desert. I have endeavoured to choose only the finest quality black and white photographs from those available to me, the majority of which appear in this book have never been published since the end of the war.

So read on and take a journey back in time to a land where Italian soldiers and colonists set off singing, on their way to build a new North African Empire.

ABOVE: Native mounted Carabinieri, or "Muntaz," Tripolitania. - Franco Festa Archives.

BELOW: Libyan "Savari" (light horse cavalry) patrol a section of the Via Balbia highway. - Ufficio Storico.

PART I
THE ITALIAN COLONY OF LIBYA

COLONIAL ADMINISTRATION

The colony of Libya was governed by a governor who was also commander of the ground, sea and air forces. He was nominated by royal decree on the proposal of the Minister for Italian Africa and confirmed by the Council of Ministers. A vice-Governor was located in Bengasi.

The governor dealt directly and exclusively with the Minister for Italian Africa and according to the instructions received from the minister directed the policy and administration of the colony, took measures for its security and maintenance of public order, and ensured the application of laws and regulations. In addition the Minister for Italian Africa could delegate to him such other functions deemed necessary by the Italian Government.

Libya was divided into four provinces and a southern military zone. Each of the provinces - Tripoli, Misurata, Bengasi and Derna was administered by a Prefect, who was central governments direct agent and representative in the province. Assisted by an administrative council, and was sub-divided into commissariats, residencies and vice-residencies.

When the colony was declared to be in a state of war, the government was invested with the powers that in similar cases were conferred on army corps commanders by the penal code for the army and by military laws and regulations.

ABOVE: Governor and Commander-in-Chief of Military Forces in Libya, Italo Balbo. He was pessimistic about the war's outcome, but he nevertheless began preparations for battle with the forces that were available to him. He was accidentally shot down and killed by Italian anti-aircraft fire over Tobruck on June 28th, 1940.

- QEII Army Museum, Waiouru, New Zealand.

ABOVE: Italian Colonial Libya, 1940.   Scale: 1:10,000,000

POLITICAL ORGANISATIONS

The Fascist Party was the single most dominant political organization in Libya.

In Tripolitania it operated under the umbrella of the Fascist Federation with a federal secretary who had under his direction four regional groups named after prominent Italians, Emilo De Bono, M. Bianchi, C. M. De Vecchi and Italo Balbo.

These groups in turn were divided into 20 sub-sections which had a total membership of 6000. The federation also included the provincial committee of the Colonial Union of Fascists which catered for artists and professionals, employers, tradesmen and labourers. There existed a commission for female Fascists which was comprised of 16 groups totaling around 850 women and also a female Fascist youth group with about 180 girls.

A university fascist group had a muster of circa 180 members. While a federal command for male Fascist youth numbered nine groups with a membership of just over 1200 members. A purely political organization for Libyan adults known as the Muslim Association of the Fascist Rod (AML) existed, this came into being on 1st December 1939 and was the brain child of Italo Balbo. The association came under the umbrella of the secretary of the Fascist Party, Achille Starace. The nominated leader of the AML, was the inspector of the Fascist Party for libya.

Only those Libyans who had been granted special (though limited) Italian citizenship by Royal Decree No.70 on 9th January 1939 were eligible to belong. The applicant for this citizenship had to be over 18 years old, to have no prison record, to have belonged to the Fascist Youth or served in the army, or to be able to read or write Italian. This citizenship was necessary for any Libyan with ambitions to rise in the military or civil organizations. The recipients were officially referred to as Moslem Italians

The aim of the association was to promote the moral and civil

ABOVE: Ettore Bastico Governor of Libya, appointed after Italo Balbo's death, from July 1941 until February, 1943. Here he is being welcomed by the Libyan population.

- Rudy D'Angelo

education of Moslem Libyans and to create a pro-Italian leadership. The association only had a brief life due to the coming of the war.

Young Libyans had the opportunity to belong to a group known as the Arab Youth of the Fascist Rod. It was called the *"Gioventu Araba Del Littorio,"* or GAL for short. It had been formed in 1935, and by 1940 it comprised eight (8) Arab Fascist Youth battalions. Of these, four (4) were composed of Arab males up to the ages of 8-15, and known as the *Aftal*. The other four battalions were made up of older Arab youths and a battalion each was stationed in Tripoli, Misurata, Bengasi and Derna. The senior, *Sciubban*, was for youths aged 16-18 years. The four Sciubban battalions together, were referred to as the Arab legion. Total strength in May 1938 was 1900 *Sciubban* and 4000 *Aftal*.

It had a philosophy and training much the same as the European Fascist Youth. It was, however, not a paramilitary formation but a political one, even though small calibre weapons were issued to the *Sciubban* during drill. The para-military portion of their training mainly consisted of marching and basic drill. They were not issued with any weapons, but used a short baton instead. The *Sciubban* did undertake training with light weapons. The GAL was solely a political organization, and it was never intended to be used in a combat role, although no parade was complete in Lybia without a detachment of Arab Fascist Youths participating. Members of the *Sciubban* undoubtedly did go on to enlist in the *Regio Corpo Truppe Coloniali della Libia* (Royal Lybian Corps of Colonial Troops), or RCTC. During WW2 many former GAL members fought with the Italians in the colonial army. This was Italy's colonial army in which the officers were Italian, although the majority of the NCO's and other ranks were Lybian.

MILITARY PROVINCES OF LIBYA

The western province of Libya, Tripolitania, was bounded on the west by Tunisia and southern Algeria and extended south to the 29th parallel. Tripoli was the principal city and port of Libya. It was the seat of the Governor-General. The new Italian designed Tripoli was complete with fine modern buildings, and blocks of apartment buildings, squares with fountains imitated from Rome, statues, palm lined boulevards and public gardens, very much in keeping with Fascism's ideals of an Imperial Roman resurgence.

The Governors residence stood in its own grounds near the cities south-eastern entrance. An old Spanish castle was used as his office, it included the police headquarters, a prison and Blackshirt barracks. A number of military barracks were located around Tripoli, among them: The Imperial barracks: Ballia barracks, which had a garage for about 500 vehicles adjacent to it; the cavalry and tank barracks at Porto Benito; the P. Verri barracks, which had an adjacent rifle range.

There was a training ground on the plain of Belaschar between Mellaha and Tagiurain on which parades and reviews were held East of Misurata, the desert region which reached the sea was known as the Sirte, oases were few and far between. This desert formed a desolate barrier between Tripolitania and Cirenaica. The eastern province of Cirenaica was bordered in the east by Egypt, in the south by Italian territory and in the west by Tripolitania. The main town and port was Bengasi. It contained the headquarters of the naval, army and airforce units stationed in Cirenaica, as well as those of the local Fascist and government organizations.

Bengasi contained a number of military barracks among them the Torelli, with housing for 1000 troops and stabling for 100 horses; the Moccagatta; the Royal Frontier Guards; Campo Eritrea (native barracks) and the Tenente Hetzel. The second largest town and port was Derna. It boasted a military airport, a naval wireless station and barracks, among them The Generale

Salso with accommodation for 300 personnel and an infirmary for 60; Sabatini Barracks; Artillery barracks and Infantry barracks.

The area of Cirenaica from the Gulf of Bomba east to the Egyptian border was called Marmarica, and - with the exception of a few regions- was extremely poor, without water and virtually devoid of trees. The most important centre was the harbour town and naval base of Tobruch. The harbour gave excellent protection and was suitable for small cruisers, light craft and submarines, and there was also anchorage for seaplanes. Tobruch had naval barracks and army, native troops and Carabinieri barracks. There was a prohibited flying zone of 9km radius around the town for civilian aircraft.

Further along the coast was the harbour of Bardia, the easternmost settlement on the Libyan coast. The harbour permitted anchorage of ships up to 4060 tonnes. Disembarkation was by lighter in fair weather. On the low ground near the harbour there were military and harbour offices and garages, plus a number of military barracks for the garrison. In the south among the oases of Gialo, Giarabub and Cufra stretched the southern extreme of the Libyan Desert, a high flat-top plain scoured by wadies and sandy dunes.

The oasis of Giarabub, which sat in the desert nearly forgotten, importantly, however, was its position on the extreme western edge of the Egyptian border. The Italians established a military post and meteorological observatory there. The portion of the Sahara Desert south of Tripolitania from the Red Desert and Black Mountains to the southern border with French Sudan and extending east to the 20th meridian was known as the Fezzan.

This vast expanse was formed by rocky plateaus 400-600 metres high, covered mainly by sand dunes, ancient wadies and interspersed with oases and water holes. A part of this was divided into the military district of the south, and consisted of a single military zone, with its headquarters in Hon, and was divided into the military sub-zones of Brach, Gat, Murzuch, Hon and El Giof, each with their own headquarters.

The military zone was bounded in the west by the line of the Algerian frontier, on the east by the line of the Egyptian and Anglo-Egyptian Sudan frontier, on the north by the southern boundary of the commissariats and on the south by the frontier with the French possessions and with Anglo-Egyptian Sudan.

THE FRONTIER WIRE

Constructed originally not as a defence but with the object of preventing Libyans from crossing unlawfully into Egyptian territory, it formed only a minor obstacle to motor transport. It stretched from the wells of el Ramleh in the Gulf of Sollum across the high plateau and the barren steppe of the Marmarica beyond Giarabub to the great sand dunes of the Sahara, a distance of 271km.

The wire cost 200,000 English pounds to construct and was said to have saved the deployment of 15 battalions along the border. The fence itself consisted of : Iron pickets 10cm diameter set on a concrete base 30 centimeters square. Height above the ground was 1.7 metres with 30cm buried. 26kg of barbed wire for every 4m of front. It was 2 stranded with pointed barbs approximately 10cm apart. Generally speaking, it was not kept in good repair.

It was watched by three main and six small guard posts. The main posts at Amseat, Scegga and Giarabub were already in existence when the fence was built, but improvements and additions were made. Amseat on the coast road had a small fort, the Ridotta Capuzzo, in which the garrison and most of the equipment was housed. It had one heavy machinegun in towers at each of the four corners. In addition there were four machinegun emplacements between the fort and the frontier wire, two on each side of the main road.

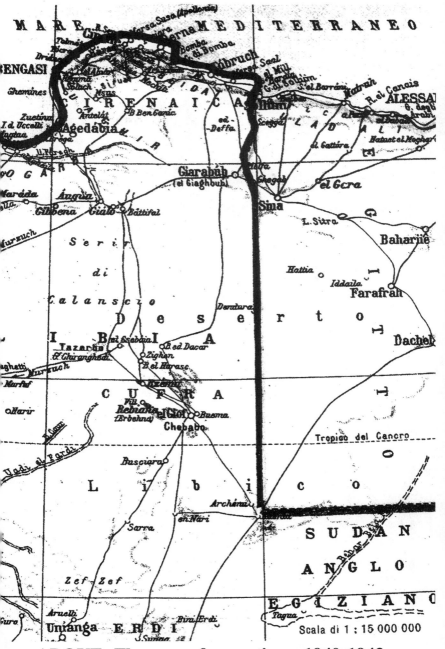

ABOVE: The area of operations, 1940-1943

ABOVE, BELOW & NEXT PAGE: Fort Capuzzo was south of Bardia, facing the Egyptian border. It was a typical desert fort of this period, with white stone walls and battlements, a central courtyard, which housed the mens quarters at its edges. Although adequate to keep tribesmen at bay, its walls crumbled against modern British artillery, which soon reduced it to a gutted rubble-strewn shell.

- Author's Collection.

RIGHT: The defences of Eastern Cirenaica in 1940. Aside from the barbed wire and the stakes embedded into concrete, a few stationary strong-points jotted the border here and there. No mine-field of any importance covered the border area at this time.

- Author's Collection.

24

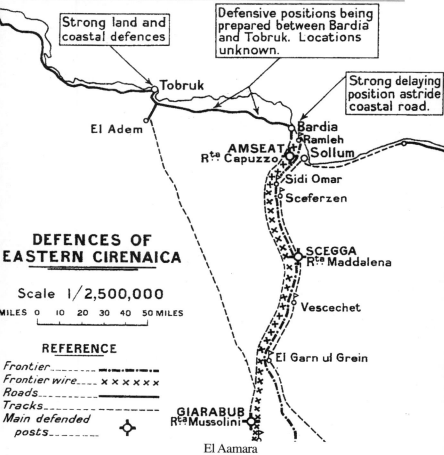

Strong land and coastal defences

Defensive positions being prepared between Bardia and Tobruk. Locations unknown.

Strong delaying position astride coastal road.

Tobruk

El Adem

Bardia
Ramleh
AMSEAT
R.ta Capuzzo
Sollum
Sidi Omar
Sceferzen

DEFENCES OF
EASTERN CIRENAICA

Scale 1/2,500,000

MILES 0   10   20   30   40   50 MILES

SCEGGA
R.ta Maddalena

Vescechet

El Garn ul Grein

REFERENCE

Frontier .... —··—··—··
Frontier wire ..... × × × × × ×
Roads .... —————
Tracks ....
Main defended
    posts ....

GIARABUB
R.ta Mussolini

El Aamara

25

There was also a landing strip for aircraft. At Segga was the Ridotta Maddalena, had a garrison of just over 100. It consisted of an oblong enclosure of barbed wire measuring 91m by 274m. Inside this were a few small buildings, and a tall trellis-work observation tower about 30m high. There were six machinegun emplacements, one each side of the four corners of the enclosure, and two on the perimeter wire. The latter were on small circular towers about 3m high. There was also a landing ground nearby.

At Giarabub was the Ridotta Mussolini, a small mud fort with 3.6m walls. One heavy machinegun was placed in each of its two towers, and two small field guns were kept inside. The fort was surrounded by three belts of barbed wire, 1.2m in height and placed close together. At the landing ground there was a stone hanger for four aircraft, and a modern workshop. The six minor posts were at Ramleh, Sidi Omar, Sceferzen, Vescechet, Garn ul Grien and El Aamara. These consisted of a fortified wall with battlements and loop holes and two machinegun emplacements in enfilade of the wire, quarters for the commander and quarters for the garrison a garage for three armoured vehicles, a small arsenal and storehouse a telephone room and a petrol store.

The whole system was connected by a telephone line which ran the length of the wire. A road parallel with the fence was used by patrols.

ABOVE: Libyan troops preparing a strong point along the frontier wire. - Antonio Munoz Collection.

BELOW: The frontier wire that seperated Libya and Egypt (known as Graziani's Wall), consisted of triple rows of metal stakes embedded into concrete, interwoven with barbed wire. It ran from the coast for 100 kilometers southward. - ATL, Wellington, New Zealand.

ABOVE: Infantry Major, circa 1941. This officer belongs to the 85th Infantry Regiment of the 60th "Sabrartha" Infantry Division. He wears the typical equipment of an infantry field officer. A khaki Sahariana tunic with baggy breeches. A sam brown belt with a model 1934 9mm Beretta pistol and high leather boots, which were sometimes substituted for ankle boots and puttees. His rank is shown on the tunic shoulder boards and also on the side of his cap which was called a Bustina. Malcolm Thomas.

PART II
ITALIAN MILITARY GROUND FORCES

ABOVE: Italian infantry in North Africa.

- Antonio Munoz Collection.

RIGHT: The Italian North African Campaign Medal.

- Keith Williams.

ITALIAN MILITARY GROUND FORCES

The land, naval and air forces of Libya came under a single Higher Command for the armed forces in Italian North Africa. The commander was assisted by a staff composed of officers from the three services. When the Governor held military rank he was the ex officio commander of the armed forces. The ground forces of Libya comprised the Royal Corps of Colonial Troops

ABOVE: A group of Libyan soldiers resting in the desert after a training mission. Among them are transport and artillery troops, who are wearing the brass branch of service badges on their fez, or Tachia. - Rudy D'Angelo.

in Libya, Formations and units of the metropolitan army and Libyan militia units.

THE ROYAL CORPS OF LIBYAN COLONIAL TROOPS

The Royal Corps of Libyan Colonial Troops was established by royal decree September 1935, whereby the previous independent colonial forces of Tripolitania and Cirenaica were abolished and a single corps substituted. Officers were normally seconded from the metropolitan army to the Colonial Corps at their own request. They could, however, be seconded without option if there was a shortage of volunteers with the necessary qualifications.

Preference was given to those on the active list, on the half-pay list, and to bachelors or widowers without family. The acceptance of married officers, if accompanied by their families, depended on the appointment for which they were required and its location. Officers were generally not accepted if they had recently returned from the colonies and had not completed one year's home service. The tour of duty was for two years, but could be extended to six. If a state of war was proclaimed could be kept on indefinitely.

Warrant officers and men for all arms, except Carabinieri, needed for the Colonial Corps were drawn from regular army troops who had applied for transfer or who were transferred compulsorily; men from the army and naval reserve with the necessary qualifications and who had applied for re-engagement in the Colonial Corps, those called up for military service in the normal way who before being drafted to units volunteered for the Corps, and Italian citizens born and resident in Libya, with military obligations to fulfill.

Carabinieri Warrant officers were drawn either from the active list or from the reserve, and from those who applied to be admit

ABOVE: *Libyan troops of the Italian North African army.*
                                               - Antonio Munoz Collection.
BELOW: *Libyan paratroopers clip their static lines in preparation for a training jump over the Castel Benito airfield near Tripoli. They are equipped with Salvator D.39 parachutes.*
                                               - Rudy D'Angelo.

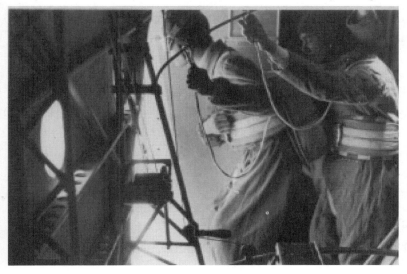

ted or re-admitted to the Carabineri or mounted police units of the Royal Corps of Colonial Troops.

The tour of duty was for three years, but could be extended for an additional two years if necessary. In addition to the ordinary colonial allowance, officers and Nco's of metropolitan troops and mobilized units of the Colonial Corps received a special payment equivalent to 25% of their pay while serving in Libya. Native troops could volunteer at the minimum age of 16, then undertake training for three months. Preference was given to natives of Libya and other Italian colonies, although those from beyond the frontiers of these colonies were accepted. Up to 1939 enlistment was voluntary, from 1940 there was a limited form of conscription introduced which was gradually tightened due to manpower shortages.

Terms of enlistment were one year for Saharan groups and two years for other units, after which a native soldier could re-engage for further periods to enable him to complete 12 years continuous service. Re-engagements could be refused or soldiers discharged through reduction of establishment, disbandment of unit or on medical grounds. Recruits for mounted units, with their own horses were provided with free forage or its equivalent value in cash. In certain cases the animal was bought by the unit.

COMBAT UNITS

The infantry was much the same as the metropolitan infantry and equipped with similar equipment and weapons. The two primary formations were the 1st Libyan Sibelle and 2nd Libyan Pescatori divisions which had artillery, engineers and support elements. There was also non divisional units such as a motorized machinegun battalion, achinegun companies, a mixed battalion of engineers and motor transport groups.

Savari were regular light horse cavalry, with squadrons stationed in Tripolitania and Cirenaica Spahis were irregular horse cavalry with rudimentary military training. They were organized into squadrons and utilized in a border patrol role Meharisti, or camel corps, were employed on police duties such as the guarding of wells, road centres and as escort to caravans.

Sahariani were the desert troops who were used for internal security of southern deserts and defence of the southern frontier, utilizing motor transport not camels. Zaptie or auxiliary native Carabinieri (military police). The training for this arm was military. Corps were chosen exclusively from Muslims and were stationed as far as possible in the districts to which they belonged. They were able to keep their families with them, and to follow their own rites and customs.

Libyan paratroops were raised in 1938 to regimental strength from Libyan volunteers, known as the 1st Regiment of Infantry of the Air, and training at Castel Benito airfield near Tripoli. But many accidents occurred and as a result it was decided to downgrade the regiment to a battalion. A second volunteer battalion comprising Italian nationals from the Royal Army, the 1st National Parachute Battalion of Libya, was formed in early 1940. A letter written by a paratrooper to a comrade gives an insight to the morale of the unit at the time:

Dear Rossi,

Whatever you may think of my postal delay is less than what I think myself. Since you left days have been far from quiet - first at Tripoli then at Castel Benito. Up bright and early as driver for the major, all the harder because I don't go to bed early either - and why? Well, I've got engaged not as usual but really this time...(a description of the lady)...who is good and so obliges me to try and be the same...

"I'm at Barce with the battalion. We practice descents awaiting the great day promised to us. We get an occasional accident just to uphold morale. I carry about my 80kg body in good health and just wait. How long now I've been waiting,

ABOVE & BELOW: *A road making crew of Italian army engineers work on a new road that was being built as a diversion around Tobruck. It took just three months to construct it, and was called the "Axis Road." This photograph was taken in 1941.*

- Dal McGuirk.

BELOW: German soldiers browse through the selection of books and magazineson sale from a mobile book shop, run by an Italian proprietor (left foreground). The Italian & German postal systems were also very much appreciated by the Axis troops. Even in the worst of times, they managed to keep the letters moving.

- Dal McGuirk

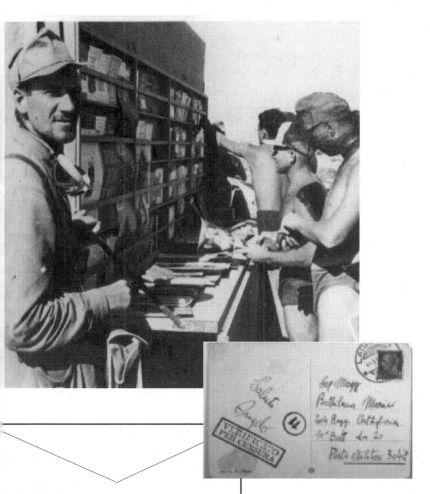

Rossi my lad!!! The war I mean, of course. I promised you a couple of English cars and I'll send them.

"Having passed to the Royal Corps of Colonial Troops we haven't had any pay, not even the war pay. We get advances by drops and so learn the joy of poverty. How goes it. Your duty is to keep your ghisbi (water bottle) clean, the ladies like it so. True?

"I've heard good news of the Libyan Battalion and know you had your part in it. Here we rot. Just imagine - an unknown parachute officer stole the harness of two Generals at the mess and they had to go home nearly naked.

"The troops, for rivalry, raid everything at night - calves, chickens and what not. Folk shut doors and windows when they are about.

"I rear my company on kicks and blows, which is the only way. Succeeds pretty well. There is every sort of belligerent in the battalion. I suppose the right kind really - they serve best in war. Do I bore you? Minelli (the bearer of the letter) will give you the latest from Tripoli.

Brachetti."

"Parachute Battalion Barce 31 July 1940."

In the defence of Cirenaica between the 15th January and 6th February 1941, the two colonial paratroop battalions, who were never used in their specialized role, were deployed as infantry with a combined unit strength of 850 men. The battalions fought bravely but were practically destroyed, suffering 185 killed, 200 wounded, and 327 captured.

SUPPORT SERVICES

Libyan Artillery services had a headquarters at Tripoli and a detached section at Bengasi with its own offices and laboratories

ABOVE: A Catholic mass is performed in the field by a military priest for personnel of the 25th "Bologna" Infantry Division.

- Author's Collection.

LEFT: A Fiat SPA CL39 truck. This small petrol powered vehicle was fitted with semi-pneumatic tires, which didn't make it a particularly comfortable vehicle to travel over rough terrain!

- Author's Collection.

Libyan Engineer services also had a headquarters at Tripoli and a detached section at Bengasi with offices and stores. Libyan Medical services: The headquarters at Tripoli included a pharmacy and medical stores depot. There was also a headquarters in Bengasi with a branch pharmacy and medical stores depot. There was also a single medical company. Libyan Supply services: Comprised a directorate with it's headquarters in Tripoli and a detached section at Bengasi. The service also had a supply company and various supply establishments.

Transport services: There was one transport establishment consisting of a headquarters with one section in Tripoli and one in Bengasi. Each had its own workshop and stores depot. There also existed non-combatant labourers organised into work battalions and companies.

HEADQUARTERS AND TRAINING ESTABLISHMENTS

The following headquarters existed for Libyan troops: One for the Royal Corps of Libyan Colonial Troops at Tripoli, in which was incorporated the headquarters of Libyan Troops of Tripolitania, artillery headquarters and engineer headquarters.

That of Libyan troops of Cirenaica was based at Bengasi; a headquarters for Libyan infantry at Tripoli and Bengasi; headquarters for Libyan cavalry at Tripoli; and a headquarters of the military territory of the south at Hon.

There was a school for Libyan NCO's at Tripoli and training schools for Libyan soldiers at Tagiura, Chersa, Barce and Bengasi. After the battle of El Alamein in November 1942 the Libyan troops had suffered heavily from casualties, prisoners and desertions. With only a diminished force remaining, the Italian Government formally disbanded the Royal Corps of Libyan Colonial Troops in January 1943.

THE SOUTHERN MILITARY COMMAND

The military command of the south embraced more than 60% of Libya This sparse land had a population density of 0.3 people per square kilometre and extended south of the 29th parallel to Libya's southern border. The region was under military law, and since 1928 the headquarters for the southern military command had been based at Hon.

The command had under its control five Auto Saharan companies, with headquarters at Hon, but were stationed chiefly at Kufra (before it was captured by the Free French), Zella, Murzuk and Sebha. There were also detachments at Jalo and Marada, but of the latter only infrequently. The companies worked in conjunction with Caproni Ca310 army co-operation aircraft. The Auto Sahara companies were the Italian equivalent of the British Long Range Desert Group in that its patrols were the only Italian mobile force operating in the desert.

The LRDG had skirmishes with detachments of the Auto Saharan Patrol and sometimes narrowly missed running into them - the Saharan vehicle tracks in the sand could always be recognized, for they included nine double-track and two single-track vehicles. The LRDG had its first skirmish with an Auto Saharan patrol on January 31, 1941, when T Patrol (New Zealand) was attacked at Gebel Sherif, losing its commander, several trucks and considerable ammunition and stores. A fortnight later there was a 10 day battle at Kufra between the Auto Saharan company stationed there and a Free French raiding party under the command of Colonel Jacques Leclerc, up from Chad. The French inflicted severe casualties on the garrison; thereafter Italian orders of battle mentioned remnants of it only.

Captain L. H. Browne of the LRDG noted in his personal diary for July, 1941:

"During July, two troops of T Patrol made a raid. The IO [Intelligence officer], Captain Shaw, had discovered a photograph

album at Kufra in which there was a photograph of a road called the Fustificato Leo, from Zella to Taiserbo. This road was constructed by Colonel Leo of the Italian Saharan command and was marked by 40-gallon drums (Fustificato is Italian for a 40-gallon drum). The were landing grounds marked along this road by letters of the alphabet, D, R, C, C' and A.

"The patrol was sent out to see if this road really did exist. They followed and mapped the course of the Fustificato Leo and examined and noted the position of each landing ground. On landing ground C' some 35,368 litres of aviation spirit were discovered and destroyed.

"The patrol was picked up by a Ghilbli and strafed and bombed and had to return to Taiserbo. The distance covered was about 1609 kilometres. There were no casualties."

Trooper Wally Rail, T1 Patrol (New Zealand) Long Range Desert Group, recalls:

"We were on patrol near Agedabia south of Benghasi. The truck I was on had just driven over the crest of a sand dune when on the other side we saw an Italian truck armed with a 20mm Breda on the back. The Italians must have seen us about the same time, but our crew was quicker off the mark and we captured the Italians. It belonged to an Auto Saharania patrol, although strangely there was only the one truck by itself. The officer in charge was a real arrogant Fascist, we took the Italians back to Siwa, but they would not talk..."

"Colonel Leclerc of the Free French coming up from Lake Chad was pushing the Italians in the deep south, northwards. We of the LRDG were patrolling in the hope of catching some of the stragglers. At Fort Saba south of Hon our lookout spotted an Italian column approaching from the south."

"We ambushed it, we shot it up thoroughly with all the firepower we possessed, though for all the shooting that went on, miraculously only one Italian was killed. We took the survi-

ving prisoners back to Hon with us..."

"On the way back from a LRDG raid on the Barce airfield on the night of September 13, 1942, we found two Italian light tanks blocking our exit. Captain Nick Wilder ordered his driver to ram one of the tanks, it shunted it out of the way but in the process destroyed his truck. We picked up the captain and his crew and carried on".

"About 7 that same morning we were ambushed in a narrow valley south of Sidi Selim by about 200 Libyan troops including cavalry. We managed to escape from that after some hard fighting. Later we were strafed by CR42 and MC202 fighter planes, which set fire to all but one Chevrolet truck and a jeep of our patrol..."

"We favoured the use of the captured Italian 20mm Breda cannons which were good guns, though the Italians did not appreciate being on the receiving end of their own weapons. We felt sorry for the Italians. I don't mean this in a patronizing way, it was just that their equipment was bad in comparison to ours (which was not that good itself). With any prisoners we took, we fed them and gave them some V cigarettes (and hoped they didn't choke on them) and put them on the heavy section trucks which brought supplies up from Cairo for the return leg, where they were handed over to military authorities as POWs."

The Italian response to LRDG incursions was never strong or concerted enough to stop them. The Italian southern command also had under its control Libyan garrison machinegun companies, Meharisti companies, Libyan engineers and a motor transport section. Artillery consisted of a battery of 20mm AA guns, and one of camel-borne pack artillery (65/17 infantry guns), with the heavier firepower provided by the frontier guards which in the main consisted of troops of 77/28 guns.

Garrisons were maintained at 15 main oases and 11 minor ones in the Sahara region. The smaller ones had Carabinieri posts and at some a small number of Libyan troops or Meharisti were attached.

THE FRONTIER GUARD

This was much the same as its parent organization in Italy in that it guarded and controlled the frontiers, except that in Libya it was also responsible for lines of communication. It was divided into sectors each of which could contain artillery, infantry and engineers The strength of each sector depended on the requirements of the particular frontier. In Tripolitania the frontier guard headquarters was in Tripoli with 28th sector at Zuara, 29th at Nalut, 33nd at Zanzur and 34th at Suani Ben Adem. In Cirenaica the headquarters was at Tobruch with the 31st and 32nd sector, the 30th sector was at Bardia, and 38th at Fort Capuzzo. Private Vito Romano of the 31st sector Frontier Guard relates:

"I was a army reservist and 21 years old when called up to service on May 6, 1940. My parents were upset that I was recalled to arms, my older brother had already been called up in August 1939 and shipped to Libya [he was a blackshirt of the 172 battalion of the 270th Legion of the 4th Blackshirt Division "3 Gennaio", and was captured at Sidi Baranni in December 1940, he ended up a prisoner of war in India and then Australia], with me gone there were no sons at home.

"I was assigned to the 4th Infantry Regiment [29th Piemonte Infantry Division] at Catania (Sicily). In early June I was embarked from Messina and transported to Libya by sea. I knew nothing about Libya before I arrived there.

"We arrived in Tripoli and were transported directly to Tobruch, where I was re-assigned to the 31st sector of the Frontier Guards around Tobruch. In early November, I was assigned to an anti-tank gun, the first one I had ever seen.

"Our duty was to escort a supply convoy to Giarabub near the

Libyan-Egyptian border, we had one truck mounted with an anti-aircraft gun, another with an anti-tank gun, while a third contained infantry support, there were also three or four vehicles loaded with supplies for the fort.

"On one escort halfway to Giarabub we were attacked by two enemy fighter planes, though they did not do any real damage.

"In early December we were under siege, no food or ammunition was able to reach us. I suffered much hunger. In mid February one of our aircraft tried to come in for a landing, the British opened fire and hit the plane, the bullets were whistling only a few centimetres above our head.

"We were captured on March 21, 1941. We were placed in a line and were marched towards English lines. I had one can of meat in my hands, though I had no way of opening it. One of the guards next to me took it from me and walked away; he returned 3-4 minutes later, and gave me the opened can. I was so happy from that moment on, I will never forget that act of kindness."

COLONIAL BLACKSHIRT MILITIA

In 1924 two legions were formed in Libya from local Italian volunteers and volunteers from Italy: The 1st Oea Legion - Tripolitania and the 2nd Berenice legion, Cirenaica, which fought the Senussi but in 1934 they were disbanded. In 1935 they were redesignated battalions, becoming part of an infantry regiment of the Cacciatori d'Africa - colonial troops of the army.

In the same year the Colonial Militia was reformed in Libya as the MVSN (Volunteer Militia for National Security) group of legions. It consisted of a headquarters, four legions based in Tripoli, Musurata, Bengasi and Derna respectively, a detachment of anti-aircraft, a detachment of coastal artillery and a depot.

There was one legion (the 10th) of the Forestry Militia based at Tripoli, responsible for the protection of forests, fisheries and

ABOVE: *Officers of the Colonial Blackshirt Militia receive instructions from senior officers. Tarhuna, Tripolitania.*

- Rudy D'Angelo.

BELOW: *Soldiers of the 1st Sahariana Battalion, attached to the Maletti Motorised Group take a break beside their Fiat AS37 truck, during the unit's advance to Sidi el Barrani, September, 1940.*

- Franco Festa Archives.

game. Also based in Tripoli was an autonomous cohort (normally battalion strength) of the University Militia, comprising of students over 18 years of age and comparable to a reserve officers training corps.

The groups were under the orders of the Commanding General of the Colonial Corps for deployment and discipline, but for all other purposes it was a normal group of the ordinary Italian militia organization. Applicants for the Libyan legions had to be between the ages of 18 and 20 years. Service was for two years and counted as conscript service in the Army.

In 1940 a fascist militia volunteer battalion was raised from the four Libyan town legions, these were not true combat units as such, but were utilized more for peace keeping duties in the towns from where they were raised. They were known as the 1st Blackshirt Battalion for Tripoli, 2nd for Misurata, 3rd for Bengasi and 4th for Derna. These units melted away just prior to their towns being occupied. Two battalions (about 500 men) of the former Colonial Militia legions were still in Libya after February 1941 in the Tripoli region.

ITALIAN AFRICAN POLICE

In 1936 the political and civil situation in parts of Italy's African colonies were far from being normalised, with Ethiopia just conquered it was an empire barely subdued. A study was made of the situation by the Ministry of Colonies and it was decided that a special body of police should be formed for the African territories (Ethiopia, Somalia, Eritrea and Libya).

After due deliberation the "Corps of Colonial Police" was officially formed on the 14th December 1936, this police body was under the umbrella of the Ministry of Colonies, where it was viewed as the armed branch of the ministry, working hand in hand with civil officials. The police title was altered to the Italian African Police or PAI in May 1939. This name change was

ABOVE: Italian African Policemen (center), speaking with German officers. The policeman on the left is armed with a Beretta M38A 9mm submachine gun, which was standard issue to the African Police.
                                                    - Otto Meyer.

brought about when four coastal provinces of Libya were incorporated into metropolitan Italy. It was felt that colonial in the title was not relevant for recently promoted provinces in Libya. So it was decided to use the more pertinent Italian African Police to cover all of Italian Africa.

The PAI was multi-functional in that they undertook road, rail, port and radiotelephonic policing duties in the colonies. This was a military organization and formed part of the armed forces of the state. It was responsible for the maintenance of law and order and for the integrity of the frontiers. It took part in both police and military operations when necessary.

The Romolo Gessi Battalon was formed in September 1941 as a mobile police formation which consisted of two motorcycle companies of Moto Guzzi 500's and one armoured car company of 10 Spa AB41's. This highly mobile force was part of a army formation known as RECAM (Reconnaissance Grouping). Being totally motorized the motorcycle companies along with the armoured cars were frequently used as escorts for the Italian High Command of Ettore Bastico and also for the commander of Armoured Group Afrika General Rommel where they were constantly on the move around the battle field.

In January 1942 the PAI was reinforced with a second company of armoured cars and another motorcycle company. It was garrisoned in Barce where it's mobile force was able to patrol along the coastal road, it clashed with the British Long Range Desert Group on a number of occasions around the Barce area. From the El Alamein battles in October-November the remaining armoured cars were engaged in rear guard actions around Sirte. While the motorcycle companies were employed in policing the flow of retreating traffic, men and materials along the coastal road, a duty they carried out until the Italian forces withdrew from Tripoli into Tunisia in January 1943.

Italian African Police Courses for the SS

Between November 18th, 1940 and March 31st, 1941, a series of three short courses were held at the Italian African Police School at Tivoli (near Rome) for selected officers and non-commissioned officers of the German SD (Sicherheitsdienst, or Security Police), on Colonial Police methods. This German interest was brought about by the vision of victory in which Germany could reclaim her lost African colonies and the resulting need to police them.

The Germans held the Italian African Police in high regard and felt that it was one branch of the Italian military that they could truly learn from. It is tragically ironic that during the period these courses were held, the Italian 10th Army was virtually destroyed in Cirenaica, with Tripolitania threatened by British forces in Libya, and in Italian East Africa, stubborn defensive withdrawals by Italian and colonial troops were taking place.

ABOVE: SS-Gruppenfuehrer Reinhard Heydrich (right) discusses the technical points of a Berretta Model 38A 9mm sub-machinegun with Italian African Police General Riccardo Maraffa (left), during Heydrich's visit to Tivoli PAI school.

- Author's Collection.

This made it look like soon there would no longer be an Italian African empire to police. At Rome, on November 18th, 1940 Benito Mussolini had made the following statement:

"Our co-operation with the Germans is real comradeship, we march side by side, the blending of the two politics becoming more and more intimate, this covers the whole field- military, economic, political, and spiritual."

The courses were held under the patronage of high ranking Italian and German personnel: the Minister for Italian Africa, General Attilio Teruzzi; The Commander of the Italian African Police Corps, General Riccardo Maraffa; And the Chief of the German SD, SS-Gruppenfuehrer Reinhard Heydrich.

A large staff of suitably qualified Italian government and military personnel experienced in colonial affairs were seconded to administer and train during the courses. The three courses had a total of 148 Germans which attended them. Each course was divided up into six sections. A myriad of subjects dealing with many aspects of life in the Italian colonies were covered in a

BELOW: A PAI Captain (Primo Ispettore) demonstrates the features of a Fiat SPA AB40 (autoblinda) armored car, used by the PAI in police duties. The photograph was taken on March 18th, 1941. Later in the year, this particular AB40 was subsequently used as the command vehicle of the First PAI Battalion sent to Africa in 1941.

- Author's Collection.

series of intensive lectures and demonstrations, which included Italian Colonial Administration - civil, political, and military policies and activities employed in East Africa and Libya; Organization of the Italian African Police in all of the African colonies; Colonial cartography; And Colonial Traditions & Customs. The students were also taken through the Italian African Museum which held a large display of artifacts from the Italian colonies. They were shown field demonstrations of PAI methods and displays of the weapons and equipment utilized by the Italian African Police.

THE ABOVE SECTION ON ITALIAN AFRICAN POLICE COURSES FIRST APPEARED IN AXIS EUROPA JOURNAL, VOLUME IV, NO.14 1998, AND WAS REPRINTED HERE WITH THE PERMISSION OF THE PUBLISHER

ROYAL CUSTOMS GUARD

The duty of the Finance Guard was the control of commerce in and through the borders of the Kingdom of Italy. From early 1926 Libyan locals were enlisted into the corps. In Libya there were two detachments- one in Tripoli and the other in Bengasi. They comprised of Italian nationals, Libyan locals and recruits from Ethiopia and Somalia.

With the outbreak of World War II, the customs guard was deployed to defend Tripoli and the coast. In 1941 the High Command sent reinforcements to Libya under the command of a lieutenant-colonel. Further reinforcements were sent in early 1942, when a company arrived from Italy and was sent to Zavia to be trained in the handling of camels. In November it was reinforced with a draft of 140 Libyans and sent to garrison the town of Zuara. The company eventually withdrew into Tunisia.

LEFT: A soldier stacks Italian manufactured 20 liter "jerry" cans full of water, which will supply the columns heading towards the front in Cirenaica.

- Ufficio Storico.

RIGHT: Bersaglieri queue for their food and wine.

- Rudy D'Angelo.

THE SUPPLY OF UNIFORMS
AND EQUIPMENT

The Libyan Military Supply Directorate was responsible for the provision of uniforms and maintained an army clothing depot at Tripoli. Four subsidiary depots were located in the same locations as the sub-depots for supplies. Every October the directorate estimated the Colonial Corps needs for the coming financial year, and submitted it to the commander of the corps, Libya, who after scrutiny passed it to the Governor for approval and funding.

Requisitions for equipment common to the metropolitan army and the Colonial Corps, and for raw materials from Italy, were transmitted to the Ministry for War. Raw materials and articles to be produced locally were dealt with directly by the Libyan directorate. At the beginning of the financial year the Minister of War ordered the transfer of funds and raw material from Italy and on arrival these were sent to the central army clothing depot for testing. If satisfactory they were dispatched to the army clothing depot at Tripoli.

LEFT: The tended orderly room of a transport unit. The vehicle parked to the right of the tent is a Spa 38R light truck.

- Author's Collection.

Articles made up in the colony were dealt with by contractors who worked to patterns provided by the army clothing department The repair of all clothing and boots was carried out on a contract basis, either by military shoe makers and tailors or by civilian firms working at tariff rates. Before 1940, the deployment of formations and units of the Metropolitan Army in Libya was dependent on the political situation. With the storm clouds gathering an influx of reinforcements was sent from Italy in support of the desert war. This flow did not decline until the end in North Africa.

INFANTRY

An Italian Infantry Division was built around a core of two infantry regiments and an artillery regiment. The bulk of Italian divisions in North Africa comprised semi-motorized infantry divisions, which could transport half its number at a time. The Italian Army was fundamentally an infantry one: with a doctrine evolved to fight in the European Alps and surrounding territory, not a conflict in the North African desert. It is interesting to note that while a Metropolitan Infantry Division contained approximately 13,000 men, Libyan and Blackshirt Divisions contained only 8,000. The biggest problem the infantry faced was the chronic lack of motorized transport. In mobile warfare non-motorized infantry could at best be used in a defensive role. This, however, had little strategic value against a motorized enemy in the open desert. A lack of sufficient anti-tank weapons at regimental level also reduced its effectiveness. Although often equipped with dated infantry weapons and equipment mostly of World War I design, the Italian infantryman could still fight bravely. Efforts were made to modernize the infantry with motor transport and two motorized divisions were formed - the 101st Trieste and the

ABOVE: SRCM Model 35 hand grenades issued to infantrymen. Italian grenades were painted red and called "Red Devils" by the Britsh. This photo was taken near Tobruk between May-June, 1941.
- Author's Collection.(above)   -Rudy D'Angelo (below)
BELOW: An artillery officer (left) and a Bersaglieri 1st Lieutenant stand in front of a large motor pool of 500cc Moto Guzzi motorcycles. These bikes were used extensively by Bersaglieri to move rapidly across the desert.

A Bersaglieri in Libya

ABOVE: An Italian Bersaglieri trooper in the North African desert, as depicted by artist, Vincent Wai (who's black and white line drawings appear throughout this book). The Bersaglieri in 1940 were in a state of transition, with many of its units switching over to trucks, although the use of the motorcycle continued, even up to the armistice of 1943, and beyond (but with less frequency).

Libyan and North African Divisions

Milizia della Libia

There were two Libyan divisions formed: the 1st "Libica," and the 2nd "Libica." Just before the beginning of the first British offensive into Cirenaica, these two divisions were reinforced by artillery batteries from the 2nd CCNN (Black Shirt) Division.

A North African infantry division had a TO&E strength (on paper) of a regular Italian formation on the European continent. The only difference was the number of motor vehicles which it was supposed to have. For example, the TO&E of a North African infantry division called on it having 398 tractors (basically for the towed artillery pieces), 249 motorcycles, and 398 other motor vehicles. It is doubtful if most had all of their TO&E numbers. The following were considered North African divisions:

17th "Pavia" Infantry Division,
25th "Bologna" Infantry Division
27th "Brescia" Infantry Division,
55th "Savona" Infantry Division
60th "Sabratha" Infantry Division,
61st "Sirte" Infantry Division
62nd "Marmarica" Infantry Division,
63rd "Cirene" Infantry Division,
64th "Catanzaro" Infantry Division (formed in 1940).

102nd Trento. However, because of the low output of the country's motor industry on the eve of World War II, and shortages of gasoline and oil stocks (the Italians had almost no natural resources of their own), plans for full mechanization of the army never came to fruition during the war.

The Fate of Some Brave Divisions in North Africa

Divisione di Fanteria "Pavia" (17) : Withdrew near the Qattara Depression and acted as rear guard for the rest of the Axis forces in that area near Alam el Nuss in late October, 1942. In early November British armored columns caught up to the division, encircled and destroyed her.

Divisione di Fanteria "Bologna" (25) : From October 23rd-31st, 1942 the division was subjected to intense aerial and ground artillery bombardment, forcing the withdrawal of the unit west of Deir el Beida on November 2nd. This withdrawal failed and the unit was smahed into pieces and destroyed. Some elements of the division reached the area south of Abu Aggag on November 5th, then to Fuka on the following day and finally to Mersa Matruh where its final remnants capitulated on November 21st, 1942.

Divisione di Fanteria "Brescia" (27) : The division was holding the El Munassib salient and was fiercely attacked beginning October 24th, 1942. It withstood the continued armored, infantry, and artillery attacks until November 4th when the enemy's armored forces forced it to withdraw, first to Deir Sha'la, and then began a retreat to Fuka, but the unit was caught and wiped out within sight of Fuka.

Divisione di Fanteria "Savona" (55) : Surrounded at Bardia, the Savona Division fought bravely in the vain hope that its men would be evacuated by sea, but this proved a chimera as it even became more and more difficult to resupply the isolated division by sea. Remnants of other units streamed into Bardia while the Savona Division acted as a safe breakwater in a sea of Allied forces, but the inevitable occurred on january 17th, 1943 when the Italian "Comando Supremo" authorized the unit's surrender before more brave men were killed in what was now a hopeless situation.

Divisione di Fanteria "Sabratha" (60) : On July 1st, 1942 the unit was involved in the attempt to sieze El Alamein. On July 10th the Allies attacked the division with force but was unable to get the unit to give up ground. Unfortunately for the division this stiff resistance depleted the unit to the point where on July 25th, 1942 it was broken up but later reformed.

Divisione di Fanteria "Sirte" (61) : In January, 1941 the unit was east of Tobruk fighting against what turned out to be superior enemy numbers. By the evening of January 8th parts of the division were surrounded and subjected to intense artillery and ground attack. The situation became critical on January 20th when the first and second line of defense in the principal regiments were overrun. By January 23rd resistance had ceased and the remaining sections of the division not yet destroyed surrendered. For its heroic defense the unit was cited in Italian War Bulletin (No.223) of the war.

ABOVE: Troops of the 2nd Libyan Division deploy their 20mm M35 Breda anti-aircraft guns ready for action at Sidi el Barrani. Their Breda's are mounted on the back of Fiat M35 all terrain trucks.

- Achille Rastelli

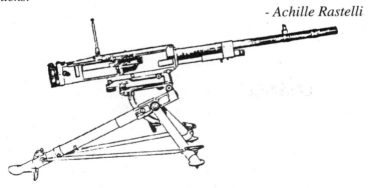

ABOVE: The Breda model 37 medium machine gun, which had a 13.8mm caliber. This weapon was gas operated, weighed 34 and 1/4 pounds and had a vertical box magazine (24 rounds). It was found throughout the Italian Army and in every theater were Italian troops were employed.

ABOVE: A 100mm (100/17) model 14 field howitzer, used to defend Tummar west camp (see text). These were ex-WWI Skoda guns built for the Austro-Hungarian Empire, which were modernised by the Italians with the addition of steel wheels and rubber rims. The gun pit the howitzer is sitting on is only half completed. This picture was dated "9 December, 1940."

- ATL, Wellington, New Zealand

BELOW: Artillerymen and their pet dog sit atop a Fiat 708 CM artillery tractor. This was produced between 1935 and 1942, and was good for towing artillery over difficult terrain, but was slow.

- Author's Collection.

61

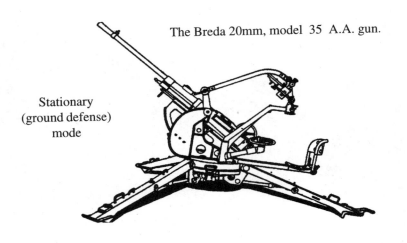

The Breda 20mm, model 35 A.A. gun.

Stationary
(ground defense)
mode

Mobile
(ground support)
mode

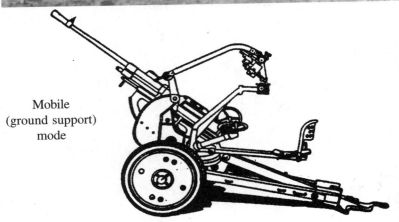

ARTILLERY

Italian artillery was distributed throughout the army and classified into three groups: divisional (field), corps (medium) and
army (heavy). The artillery had a reputation in North Africa for
accurate shooting and tenacity in action, and its troops lived up
to their motto: *"We are always in every place."*
The Italians tended to have their artillery positioned well forward, which often resulted in high casualties for gunners. The
guns used were of a mixed type, consisting mainly of World
War I Italian and Austrian pieces. The numerous calibers and types
of ammunition were a continual logistic nightmare. The need to retain
virtually obsolete weapons was the result of the inability of the
country's arms industry to produce sufficient modern artillery. Sergeant Ted Burbery, A company, 23 Battalion, 2nd New Zealand
Division recounts this episode

*" In late 1941 our company had taken up position around
Gazala, I was stationed near a very large captured Italian
ammunition dump, there were numerous types and calibre's
of shells piled high all around, there was just enough room
between them for a truck to be driven.*

*"Three of our men had acquired some Italian hand grenades
and the fools were throwing them at each other. Soon after
there was a terrific explosion, one of the piles of shells had
been detonated by a hand grenade, the resulting explosion
killed two and badly wounded the third soldier, it also left a
crater big enough to drive a three ton truck into. To play the
fool in an ammunition dump was an act of stupidity beyond*

*LEFT: The 20mm, model 35 (Breda) anti-aircraft gun. It is seen here
being manhandled by Italian troops. The muzzle velocity was 2,750 feet
per second. Maximum effective ceiling (in the AA mode) was 8,200 feet,
while the effective range in the ground support role (infantry support) was
6,000 yards. Rate of fire was about 220 rounds per minute.*
                                        - Antonio Munoz Collection.

ABOVE: A spiked 105/28 (105mm) long range howitzer. These were considered the backbone of the Italian artillery. They were built through an Ansaldo license acquired from the French firm which designed and built theSchneider 105 model 1913. The range of the Italian version was 13,250 meters. This particular gun had the newer type wheels with rubber tires fitted. It belonged to the Ariete armored division, and was captured at Alam Nayil, Egypt in an action against the 19th Battalion/ 2nd New Zealand Division on July 3rd, 1942.   - ATL, Wellington, New Zealand.

BELOW: A 152/37 artillery piece in transport mode, towed by a Breda 32 artillery tractor. These 152mm artillery pieces were captured Austrian WWI Skoda guns and were refurbished by the Italians in the 1920's with the addition of new wheels, liners and chambers. The range of this type of gun was 21,840 meters.   - Author's Collection.

comprehension."

Artillery Second Lieutenant Giovanni Bonaccio attended the reserve officer's school in Bra and Venaria Reale (near Torino). His mother was a widow and he an only son, meaning he could have easily obtained a deferral from army service being the only son of a widow. Instead, he volunteered, being proud of his Italian spirit.

In 1939, he was recalled into the army for summer manoeuvres in the western Alps.

He was first assigned to the Sforzesca Division (which was later sent to Russia as part of the Italian expeditionary forces), but was later shipped to North Africa. He would later say that was his lucky day, as he would never have endured the terrible cold of the Russian winter. On May, 24, 1941, as a lieutenant, he left home for the North Africa front. He reached Naples by train and then, on the transatlantic liner Conte Biancamano, crossed the Mediterranean to Tripoli.

His first assignment in Tripoli was with the Batteria Brighenti, part of the 30th Coastal and Anti-Aircraft Group. Later he was commander of a battery of anti-aircraft heavy machineguns (20mm Bredas) of the Pavia Division he served from Tripoli to Bengasi, Tobruch, Sollum and Mersa Matruh, until the halt at El Alamein.

Following this battle, in the first few hours of the retreat, he returned towards the enemy searching for soldiers he had lost contact with and was taken prisoner by New Zealanders. During his years in Africa when he could find the time, he wrote letters to his fiance in Italy, four of which are reproduced here:

"Tripoli, August 19, 1941.

"...In my last letter I told you I was going to dress up for an invitation to dinner at the "fattore" [Italian farmer-settler]. However, more important things happened in the meantime,

(continued on page 75)

ABOVE: Colonel Bonfante (center), the commander of the 43rd Artillery Regiment of the 61st "Sirte" Infantry Division.
                              - Franco Festa Archives.

LEFT: An R.F.2 radio set, being used on the Sollum front, in Egypt (September 3rd, 1941). This type of set was used by artillery units.
  - Rudy D'Angelo

LEFT: Artillery Lieutenant Giovanni Bonaccio, of the 7th Battery, 30th Coastal and Anti-Aircraft Group at the Sea Fort, Tripoli (July 1941).

-Riccardo Bonaccio

Of all the arms in the Italian Army, the artillery branch was most likely the best trained of all. The following are the principal pieces used:

TYPE	CALIBER (mm)	MAX RANGE (meters)
Light		
65/17	65mm	6,800 m
75/18	75mm	9,400 m
Field		
75/32	75mm	12,500 m
100/17	100mm	9,260 m
Medium		
105/28	105mm	13,200 m
Heavy		
149/12	149mm (mod.14)	6,580 m
149/35	149mm (mod.10)	9,690 m
149/40	149mm (mod.35)	21,950 m
210/22	210mm (mod.35)	16,000 m

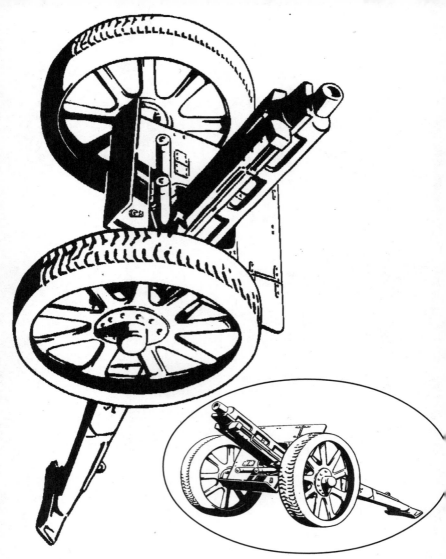

ABOVE: This gun was a 75/27 (75mm) artillery piece, model 1912. The muzzle velocity was 1,730 feet per second, and the weight of the projectile was 14 pounds. The maximum range of this World War I era gun was 11,000 yards. With a veteran (trained) crew, this gun could have a maximum rate of fire of 20 rounds per minute.

ARTILLERY PIECES EARMARKED FOR RUSSIA AND THEIR USE IN NORTH AFRICA

Guns that had been specially prepared for employment in the extreme cold conditions of the Russian Front had been specifically adapted to retain the heat of the round as it was fired by the guns. This heat, which in normal artillery pieces would have dissipated after each round would go off, was retained by these pieces, and the heat would keep the gun from freezing.

Unfortunately, at least one shipment of these specially outfitted artillery pieces were sent to the North African front. The terrible results were that, to the shock and horror of the Italian artillerymen, these guns would jam after firing only one round! Needless to say, these guns were basically useless and a total waste of the extreme expense incurred in shipping them!

RIGHT: Artillery Lieutenant G i o v a n n i Bonaccio of the Pavia Division, atop the same d e s t r o y e d Matilda (Mark II) tank at El Mechili.

- Riccardo Bonaccio

ABOVE: A captured Chevrolet 30cwt lorry used by members of an anti-aircraft battery of the 17th "Pavia" Division. Mersa Matruh, Egypt. September 14th, 1942.
      - Riccardo Bonaccio.

BELOW: Artillery officers pictured in the spring of 1942 beside a Spa TL 37 light tractor. These vehicles were used to tow artillery pieces.
      - Bundesarchiv, Koblenz.

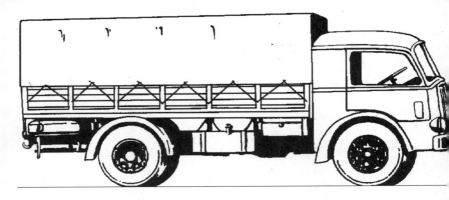

ABOVE: The Italian Fiat 666NM (4x2) military truck. This vehicle was used throughout the Italian army and photos showing Italian mules and horses being carried on these vehicles were taken in Russia. After the Lancia 3/Ro truck, the Fiat was the next most useful heavy truck in the Italian army inventory.

ABOVE: The Italian Lancia 3/Ro military truck. This vehicle was the heavyweight of the Italian motorized inventory. It was favored by artillerymen as well as by all other branches of service as a reliable and rugged vehicle with a high towing capacity.

The Workhorse of the Italian Army: The Lancia 3/Ro Military Truck

This versatile heavy truck was used on all fronts by the Italians during World War II, and was easily recognisable because of its squat square nose with a large inertia electric (6 volt) starter unit sitting beneath the radiator grill. The heart of the Lancia was a compact though powerful 93 brake horse power, 5 cylinder diesel engine (made under licence from Junkers of Germany), designated the Type 102. The truck came in two versions one with solid rubber and the other with pneumatic tires. With a double set of wheels at the back and single pair at the front, the truck had rear wheel drive. The large tray could carry up to 40 soldiers with full equipment. Because of its impressive payload capabilities and powerful engine, it was utilised for a multiple of functions, such as a water carrier (with a tank capacity of 5,000 litres), a mobile workshop, a horse transporter (animal trains were still an important aspect of the Italian military even in the days of the internal combustion engine) an ambulance, and as a tank transporter for medium tanks and Semovente self propelled gun carriages. Aside from its numerous transport roles. The large steady tray was considered an ideal platform for two different variations of mobile gun mounts. The first was a 100/17 howitzer (maximum range 8,400 yards) mounted on the tray, this WW1 period artillery piece manufactured by Terni-Ansaldo was used with a 3/Ro combination operationally in North Africa.

Another North African variant was the adoption of the powerful 90/53 anti-aircraft/anti-tank gun (19,100 feet maximum vertical range, maximum horizontal range 39,300 feet), on the 3/Ro tray. This weapon had modified fold out legs attached to support the gun platform while in the firing position. After the Italian Armistice of the 8th September 1943, the Germans seized all the available vehicles and put them into Wehrmacht service, among the tasks the 3/Ro undertook for it's new masters was as a tow tractor for the German 88mm anti-tank gun. The Lancia also found service in the reformed army of the Fascist Social Republic in Northern Italy (*Re

publica Sociale Italiane).
Approximately 9 units of all versions of the 3/Ro were manufactured of this truly classic military work-horse.

Technical statistics:

Climbing ability: 26% maximum incline.

Engine: 5 cylinder 93 bhp diesel

Transmission: 4 speed.

Brakes: Mechanical cable on all wheels.

Length: 7.25 metres.

Width: 2.35 metres.

Height' 3 metres.

Weight (empty): 5,610 kilograms

Fuel consumption: 100 kilometres per 28 litres.

Range: 500 kilometres.

Speed: Maximum 45 kilometres per hour.

The Lancia 3/Ro Military Truck was favored by Italian troops throughout the army, but was extremely liked by the artillery troops for its capacity to haul the heaviest of guns. When the Italian artillery men moved their 149mm artillery pieces, they were usually hauled by Lancias'

*our homes, where everything is an avalanche of memories,
then, more than ever, I am happy to be here to give the enemies a good hiding.*

*"Imagine that, among the papers the Tommies left behind, I
found postcards already prepared with Christmas greetings
from Tripoli!! Instead of Tripoli they got...Waterloo!*

"July 4, 1942.
"My dearest Grazia,
*"I have too many letters to answer, but I did not have the time
to do it up to now.*

*"Our advance is a run; it is a continuous fight and so, how to
write?...I imagine your anxiety while you read the war bulle-
tins and the newspapers. My division, your Giovanni, are
among the first troops.*

*"Bir Hacheim, Ain El Gazala, El Adem, Tobruch, Mersa
Matruh, Sidi Omar are all actions in which we took part, just
to name a few. Now we are well into Egypt. May God protect
our army and give us the so much longed for peace...*

*"...The night of June 28 was terrible. The division's command
was held by the undersigned because I was the only officer
left. We captured 86 of the enemy, 4 vehicles!...If there were
only the British it would be nothing. But there are Indians
(with such long knifes!!), Blacks, Chinese, French and New
Zealanders.*

*"They have all the comforts! On the front line they even have
"Ladies". At El Adem, we captured two of them...SHIT!"*

"Zone of Operations, August 1, 1942.
*"...I have been hospitalized in Barce and now I am returning
to the zone of operations. It has been a trip of thousands of
kilometres on roads that are not always perfectly paved. On
our way back, we stopped in Beda Littoria where, miracle of
all miracles, there is a restaurant with waiters dressed in tail-*

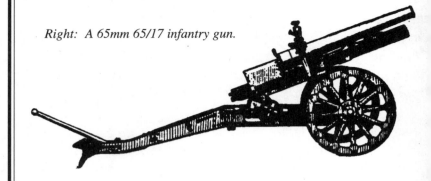

Right: A 65mm 65/17 infantry gun.

NOTES ON THE 65/17 INFANTRY GUN

This was a close support light field gun used by the Italian army. It was used in infantry and in Alpini divisions. In Italy it was normally horse towed, while in the Libyan desert, it was carried or towed by truck. The Alpini normally carried it broken down into five pack loads to be transported on the backs of mules.

It was designed at the Terni arsenal. The gun was 11' 8" long with a box tail, weighed 570 kg in firing position, and normally had a rather large shield in the front, about 4mm thick. It had spoked wheels of 3' 2" in diameter. The barrel was a 65mm caliber and used high explosive shells, which weighed 9.15 lbs. The gun also used armor piercing shells that weighed 9.3 lbs. The maximum range of the gun was 5,500 yards, though the effective range in army handbooks was stated to be 1,100 yards.

When used as an anti-tank gun, it was reported to be only effective at ranges of 550 yards or less against medium tanks. It had a maximum rate of fire of 20 rounds per minute, although five rounds per minute was the normal rate. In Libya, the gun was used extensively in an anti-tank role. It was organized there in the infantry regiments in four gun batteries manned by artillery personnel. It's reported normal establishment was four officers and 127 other ranks. By the beginning of the war, the gun was in the process of being replaced in the infantry divisions by the 47/32 anti-tank guns, which were more effective.

ABOVE & BELOW: The 47mm anti-tank gun. In this photo below, we see the breach end view of the 47/32 model 35 anti-tank gun- this one manned by members of the (fully motorized) "Giovani fascisti" Regiment. The 47/32 was the standard (principal) close support and anti-tank weapon of the Italian army. The weapon could be towed or trucked. It fired both an armor piercing round with a maximum range of 6,949 meters, and a high explosive round with a range of 3,474 meters.

- Author's Collection.

PREVIOUS PAGE: A 77/28 model 5/8 cannon sits in a well constructed gun pit. It's crew is preparing to fire against an enemy column. The 77/28 was a Skoda 76.5mm model 05/08 gun from World War I. The barrel was made from wrought bronze, while most, if not all of the ammunition for this piece was produced before the start of World War I!

- James Burd.

two enemy aircraft last night "lost their feathers". During the day we have already seen many aircraft crash, but never before during the night. It had been a thrilling experience. Usually, during the night, you just hear the noise of the aircraft and you feel their presence by the falling of the bombs and luminous lights. But, up to now, we had never caught one of them in our searchlights.

"Last night, the searchlights suddenly caught two of these enemy "boobies". You can imagine the hurricane of shots: burst of bombs, thousands of tracer bullets from the machineguns... We were all seized by enthusiasm, everyone was yelling like at a football match...I will never forget those two minutes (that was about length of time the action took place). They will compensate for all the other moments spent on this rock, listening to the explosion of the bombs a few metres away

"Last nights action was sufficient to allow us to forget all the hardship, all the sacrifices for which, many times, we called this world a bastard.

"But war is such a bad thing! If we think the British were in those two planes, then no pity! but if I think they were people just like us and I knew it was a matter of seconds and they would be shot down, then I cannot but pray to God that a fast and full victory be granted to our army..."

"February 1942

"Now the tents are set up with all the comforts: camp-beds, floor mats, chairs and many trinkets we found in the Tommies' encampments. But these are all household articles they took from the settlers' houses. How bad is war! I, for example, among other things, have a beautiful stuffed chair with its cover and I can't look at it without thinking about its original owner who had covered it in order not to ruin it! When I think about what has happened here, and could have happened to

ABOVE: An officer and troops of the South African Police Regiment examine, with great interest, a captured Breda (20mm) 20/65 model 35 anti-aircraft gun at Bardia, in January 1942.
- South African National Museum of Military History.

BELOW: Two captured, truck-mounted (75mm) 75/27 CK anti-aircraft / anti-tank guns, mounted on a Ceirano CMA50 truck chassis. This combination first appeared in 1927. This picture was taken at Sidi el Barrani, in December 1940. *- Author's Collection.*

*coats (sheer madness!!). On an immaculate table cloth we
had a Rissotto, a roast-beef with tomato salad that I will never
forget for the rest of my life. After lunch, we decided that life,
after all, was not as bad as we thought when we were under
artillery fire... From Beda Littoria, Apollonia, Luigi di Savoia
and so on, there is an enormous amount of huge public works
built here, as if by miracle, in the middle of the desert...*

*"I am serene, calm and I feel quite good, and in 3-4 days I
will be back at my anti-aircraft machineguns, just in time,
I do hope, to box the British. But, whoever saw the British in
the battle? We have seen French soldiers, Poles, Blacks, New
Zealanders, Australians, but very few British.*

*"If they had to fight as Italians and Germans fight (and
what a race of fighters are these ones), today Alexandria
would already be 500 kilometres behind our back..."*

ARMOR

The Italians classified their tanks in the following manner: L
(Leggero - light), M (Medio - medium) and P (Pesante-heavy).
The first category comprised vehicles up to 8.1 tons, the second
from 8.1-15.2 tons and the third more than 15.2 tons; Although
there were no heavy tanks available to the Italians for use in
North Africa, a tank of 26.4 tons, the P40 was produced but did
not see service before the September 1943 Italian-Allied armistice.

The tank type was designated by the appropriate letter followed
by the weight figure. The addition of the last two figures of the
year of adoption is a further conventional distinguishing mark,
ie. L 6/40 or M 11/39. Two Armored Divisions fought in Libya, the
132 Ariete and the 133rd Littorio. German Field Marshal Erwin
Rommel held the Ariete in very high esteem. An Italian armored
division was originally envisaged as a mobile reserve used to break
through the front line, utilizing shock action and the firepower

to obtain a decisive victory. It was designed to operate in conjunction with infantry or motorized divisions. As the war progressed the Italians adopted German armoured doctrines which markedly improved their tactical efficiency.

Organisation of the armored divisions was in a permanent state of development as battle losses were quickly replaced with what was available and the introduction of new equipment. By late 1941 an armoured division was a mixture of armor, artillery and infantry, consisting of approximately 8,600 men and 189 medium tanks.

In addition there were also a number of light and medium tank battalions attached to various non-armored units. The tank soldiers fought bravely, even though they faced increasingly heavier armoured and better-gunned enemy tanks, while their own inadequate armour and firepower did not markedly improve at the same pace. Sergeant Sergio Tamiozzo of the 8th Bersaglieri Regiment, Ariete Armoured Division recounts:

"I volunteered for the army and joined up on October 1, 1940. I was assigned to the 8th Bersaglieri Regiment in Verona. After two months training, on Christmas Day 1940 my regiment left in the snow for the North African front. I was happy and proud to be leaving for the front and felt that since Italy was now at war I had to do my part.

"On January 22, 1941, the 8th disembarked at Tripoli. We then spent a month in Tagiura patrolling the various oasis and manning advanced posts.

"Rommel and the Afrika Korps arrived soon after. Not long after that we started to advance. We soon had our first contact with the enemy, and a comrade of mine, who came from a town near me was our first causality in combat. He was shot in the chest and ran for about 15 metres and then fell down dead.

"We were equipped with Moto guzzi motorcycles that had a light machinegun mounted on the handlebars. We pursued the

British for three or four days and had very little to eat. I only had two cans of meat, some biscuits and a litre of water that lasted me five days. We finally halted between the forts R7and R6 in front of Tobruck.

"After three days of artillery fire we were attacked by Australians and Indians. The last memory I had of that night was a mortar shell that hit one of our 47/32 anti-tank guns about 20 metres to my right. There were explosions, shouts and curses.

"I jumped out of my foxhole and ran to the emplacement that was hit, and saw half a dozen Australians running in my direction. I threw my last Balilla (grenade) and I used the body of a dead Bersagliere as a shield. I remember rifles firing and bayonets going into flesh...hot blood... mine or my dead comrades?

"After that, all was black. When I woke up I was surrounded by five male nurses who I knew well - they were all from my home town of Valdagno and the doctor was Captain Girolamo Marchetti. Was I dreaming? No, we were all alive!

" I was in Field Hospital number 157 of the Ariete Division. From there I was transferred to the hospital Principe Di Piemonte at Derna. Where apart from my wounds I was also suffering scurvy.

"(I found out later that Captain Marchetti was taken prisoner with his hospital during December 1941 and was a prisoner of war in Egypt. He was later repatriated in May 1943 during a prisoner exchange).

"After eight days in Derna I was sent to a hospital in Bengasi and a month later I was sent home: I was then transferred to the 3rd Bersaglieri where I had the rank of sergeant."

Corporal-Major Giorgio Lupi, 3rd Group 105/28, 132 Motorized Artillery Regiment, Ariete Armoured Division, comments: *"I was conscripted when I was 20 years old and did my initial training with the 151st Infantry Regiment, 12th Sassari Divi-*

sion. Our training was based on the 1914-18 war - the lessons of Ethiopia and Spain were not yet translated into training for the troops. The mentality of the cadres was not ready for the blitzkrieg. I don't think our weapons and equipment were really adequate for the desert and war of movement.

"I was flown to Libya on May 19, 1942, in a Savoia Marchetti aircraft and we landed at Castel Benito airport, Tripoli. I did know something about Libya before I arrived, as it was in the news for the economic development and transfer of farmers from Italy. Also the big public works programmes, new towns and roads (Via Balbia)

"I was a specialist attached to a repair and maintenance support crew. We had a truck specially fitted for the recovery of broken down vehicles. We sometimes gave mechanical support to the tanks, I think the tankers were good soldiers, though in steel caskets. Our artillery was considered excellent by the experts, though in practice, especially in the desert and off road, the armoured plates in front required repetitive welding, often difficult to perform in the field. When necessary the front plates were taken off but I think this was done by initiative of the officer in charge, without permission from headquarters."

"Morale was good, though there was the usual belly aching which was limited to a few issues concerning the disparity of treatment between officers and troops due to the old mentality pervading the army. As for our leaders in Italy, they were symbols of the fatherland, tradition, state and race. Too far away from common mortals in the sand of the desert. Mussolini was considered an energetic and charismatic leader unable, however, to fight against the influence of the monarchy and church.

"I was a young soldier not converted to idealize the hierarchy of the army and its rule by the book. As an example. We were retreating at full speed, perhaps a couple of hours ahead of the 8th Army vanguard, and at Bengasi we went to the huge army depot there to refuel and get food. In this massive deport, already under siege by the Arab looters, an Italian officer ran toward us with his revolver pointed at us, ordering the unloading of the foodstuff we took without permission because 'he was responsible for the depot and every supply required had to have an order by the commandant of the unit requiring the stuff'. Under those circumstances this was a pure bureaucratic madness, typical however of the mentality of those who went by the book.

"I was with the Ariete at the Depression of El Qattara, south of the road to Alexandria, at the end of October 1942 when we were engaged in the big battle of El Alamein. From then on the events happened quickly always on the move, always on the alert, pursued on the back and on the left. I employed the usual cunning instinct of a soldier trying to survive in a hostile environment and outfoxing the foxes. The division was destroyed and we survivors were placed with other units without tanks. But we managed all the same to endure what was said to be the longest retreat in history (after that of Xenophon of the Anabasis, I suppose)."

ABOVE: A gully full of L3/35 tankettes captured when Tobruk fell, January 1941.

- ATL, Wellington, NZ

ABOVE: A front view of an L3/35 tankette. These had a crew of two (driver and gunner), with an armament of two 8mm machineguns. The vehicle was powered by an inline 4-cylinder petrol engine.

- Bundesarchiv.

BELOW: An L3/35 crew bring in a prisoner and a Morris A.C.9 armored car from the 11th Hussars, October-November 1940 (Sidi el Barrani).

- Author's Collection.

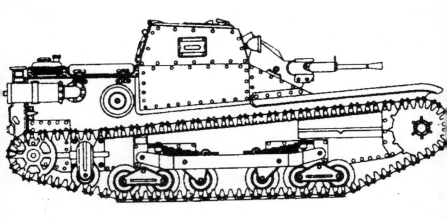

ABOVE: The L3/35 tankette. This armored fighting vehicle weighed 3.5 tons and had a top speed of 42 kilometers per hour, with a maximum range of 150 kilometers. This vehicle carried either two (2) Fiat 14/35 or Breda 8mm machine guns.

BELOW: A group of L3/35 tankettes most probably part of the LXIIIrd Battalion that got disabled when they were trapped on the salt pans between the road and the sea, during a skirmish at Buq Buq, Cirenaica, December 11-12, 1940.

- Author's Collection.

ABOVE: Two destroyed Italian tankettes above lower Bardia and Bardia Bay, Libya. This photo was taken on January 5th, 1941. The front vehicle shown here is a very rare field modified CV33 L3 which has had a Swiss Solothurn S.18/1000 20mm anti-tank rifle installed. Rocks have been added to the front chassis for extra protection. Behind this modified tankette is a CV35 L3.

- ATL, Wellington, New Zealand.

BELOW: The L3/35 tankette.

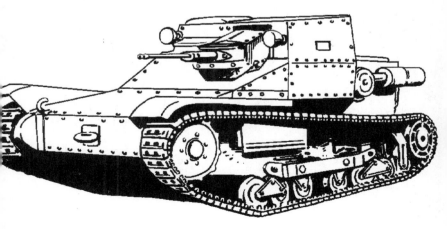

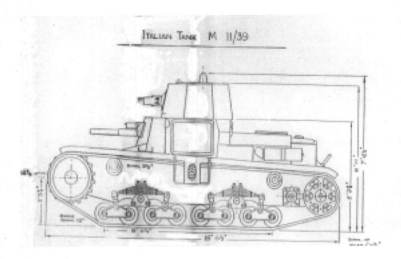

ITALIAN TANK M 11/39

ABOVE & BELOW: The M11/39 tank. It was built as an interim replacement for the Fiat 3000 tank in 1939. It was powered by a 105 hp v8 water cooled diesel engine. The main gun was a sponson mounted 37/40 for which was carried 84 shells on board the tank. Its secondary armament was two 8mm Breda machineguns in the turret. Frontal armor was 30mm thick, while the side armor was 14mm. The cross-country speed was a pitiful 9mph!. On a paved road, the tank could manage 20mph. Seventy of these tanks were sent to North Africa.   - Author's Collection.

THE M11/39 TANK

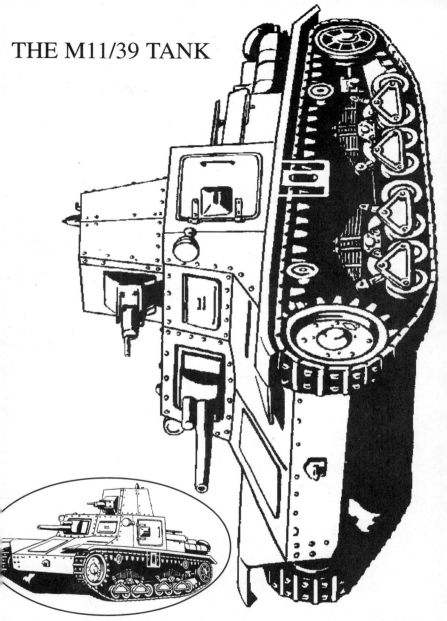

ABOVE: The M11/39 tank. The tank weighed 11 tons and had a maximum range of 210 kilometers, with a speed of 32 kilometers per hour on a paved road. Cross country, it's speed was only 9 miles per hour.

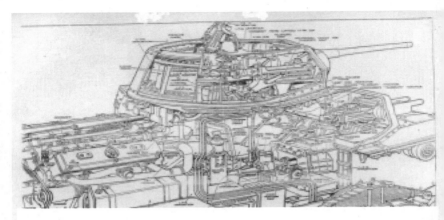

ABOVE & BELOW: The M 13/40 tank. Considered the best medium tank that the Italians fielded. Although the speed was still the same as that of the M 11/39 (20mph on a paved road, and 9mph cross-country). The significant points of improvement were the added armor: 42mm of armor thickness in the front vs. the 32mm of the M 11/39 tank. The biggest change was the 47mm gun that the M 11/40 carried in its turret. The M 11/39 only had a 37mm anti-tank gun which was useless except against soft-skinned targets or armored cars. The M 11/40, while not considered very good, was at least a marked improvement over the other "tanks" in the Italian North African inventory. The "Ariete" Division was outfitted generously with this vehicle. Below, a tank of the "Ariete" in Tobruck.

ABOVE: The M14/41 tank. The tank had extra links on the front to boost its protection against hostile anti-tank fire. The photograph (above) was very likely taken at El Alamein in November, 1942.

- Author's Collection

BELOW: The M13/40 tank. There was not much difference between both of these armored fighting vehicles

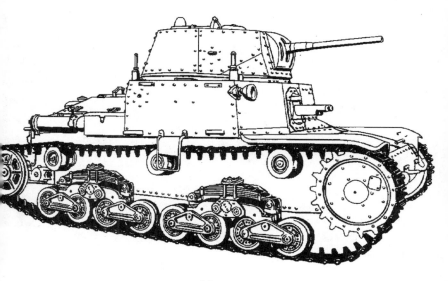

ABOVE: Three M14/41 medium tanks lead a column of armor from the 132nd Ariete Armored Division along a desert road. At the head of the column is a Fiat 508 C.M. staff car, followed by a motorcyclist.
BELOW: M13/40 medium tanks (very similar to M13/41 tanks) were the main armored fighting vehicle of the newly arrived Ariete Armored Division.

- Bundesarchiv.

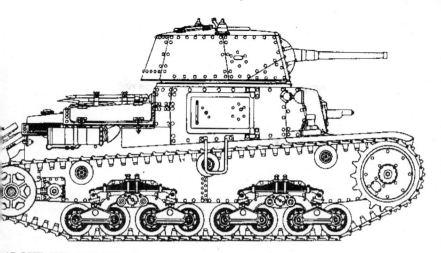

ABOVE AND BELOW: The M13/40 medium tank had a crew of four. Its main armament was a 47mm 47/32 anti-tank gun, with one coaxial 8mm Breda Model 38 machinegun in the turret, with two 8mm coaxial machineguns in the front chassis (hull), and one 8mm mounted on the top of the tank for anti-aircraft protection (although this last machinegun was not always present). The photo below is of a tank from the VIIth Tank Battalion.

- Dal McGuirk.

ABOVE: The left side of an M13/40 tank chassis. The wound is an exit hole blown out by the shell of a British 2-pounder anti-tank gun. The armor failed in this particular case, and the rivets cannot be to blame, as was so often the complaint. Italian tanks were considered by many as mobile coffins. Italian tank crews were among the bravest men in World War II who, even knowing the terrible risks, still went out to do battle in these "coffins."
- Author's Collection.

BELOW: The AB41 Armored Car, which made its appearance in North Africa in January 1941.

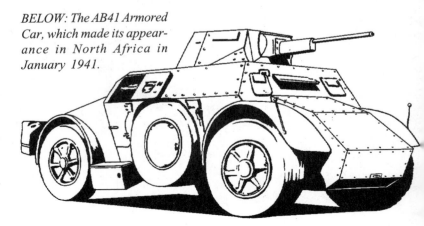

BRIGATA CORAZZATO SPECIALE

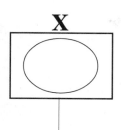

ARMOR COMPLIMENT:
25 L-3 tankettes, 57 M 13 tanks, 22 M 11 tanks, 10 Autoblinada 40 armored cars.
ARTILLERY:
three batteries of 100mm heavy artillery guns and three batteries of 75mm artillery guns.

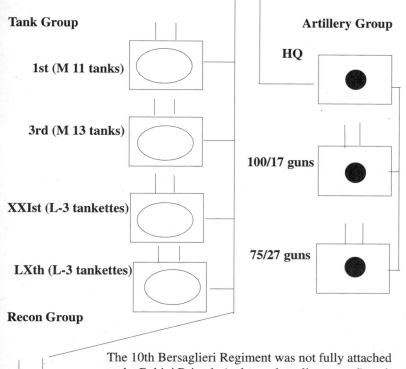

Tank Group

1st (M 11 tanks)

3rd (M 13 tanks)

XXIst (L-3 tankettes)

LXth (L-3 tankettes)

Recon Group

Artillery Group

HQ

100/17 guns

75/27 guns

The 10th Bersaglieri Regiment was not fully attached to the Babini Brigade (only one battalion served), as it was an army reserve in North Africa. It arrived in Libya in the 1st week of December, 1940 and was composed of the XVIth, XXIVth, & XXXVth battalions. Destroyed at Beda Fomm, it was to be rebuilt in Italy in 1943. One battalion served in the Babini.

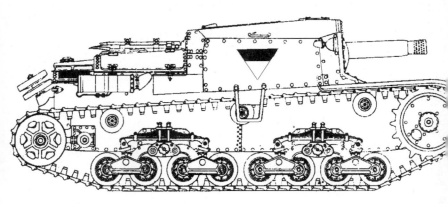

ABOVE & BELOW: The Semovente 75/18 self-propelled gun. It was armed with a 75mm field howitzer, whose combat range was 9,560 meters. This armored fighting vehicle was also armed with one Breda 8mm model M38 machine gun. The markings on the side of the hull designates this vehicle as belonging to the 5th Semovente Group of the Ariete Armored Division. It was transported by road on a heavy trailer. The photo below was taken in July, 1942.

- *Bundesarchiv.*

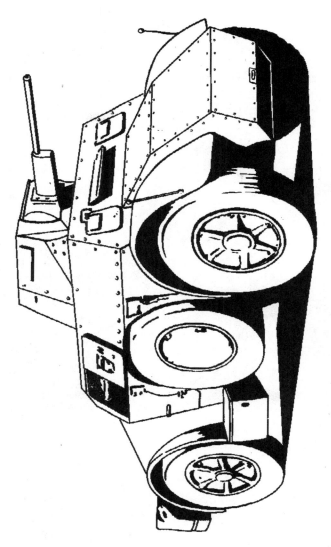

ABOVE: The autoblinda AB41 armored car. These first appeared in combat units in Africa in September 1941. They had a dual steering system, a crew of four (two drivers, commander/gunner, and a rear hull gunner). The turret was the same as that of the L6 light tank, and had a 20mm Breda cannon as the main armament. Its secondary weapon was the front and rear mounted 8mm machine guns.

Next Page Photo Credit - Bundesarchiv.

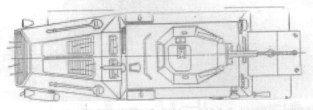

ITALIAN ARMOURED CAR
AUTOBLINDA 40

ABOVE & RIGHT:
The AB41 Armored
Car.

*RIGHT: The L6
Light Tank.*

Italian
Armored Fighting Vehicle
Specifications

NAME	WEIGHT	ARMAMENT	SPEED
M11/39	11 Tons	1 X 37mm gun/ 2 X MG's	20 mph
M13/40	13.5 Tons	1 X 47mm gun/ 3 X MG's	20 mph
M13/40	14 Tons	1 X 47mm gun/ 3 X MG's	20 mph
L6/40	6.8 Tons	1 X 20mm guns/ 1 MG	26 mph
L3/35	3.5 Tons	2 X MG's	26 mph
AB40	6.5 Tons	2 X MG's	46 mph
AB41	7.0 Tons	1 X 47mm/ 1 MG	42 mph

	FRONTAL ARMOR	SIDE ARMOR
M11/39	30mm	14.5mm
M13/40	40mm	25mm
M13/40	42mm	25mm
L6/40	40mm	15mm
L3/35	14mm	8.5mm
AB40	18mm	10mm
AB41	18mm	10mm

BELOW: Autoblinda AB41 armored cars.

- Antonio Munoz Collection.

PARATROOPS

Paratroopers of the 185th Folgore Parachute Division numbering 2676 had arrived in North Africa by mid-July 1942, the remainder of the Division arrived in early August. Originally earmarked for the invasion of Malta, it was sent to Africa when this operation was canceled. Their transport and heavy equipment arrived at the El Alamein front line during September, where these elite airborne troops were assigned as infantry.

They never got the opportunity to operate in their specialization (they left their parachutes in storage at Derna) and were obliged to fight as ordinary infantry. A large percentage of the division

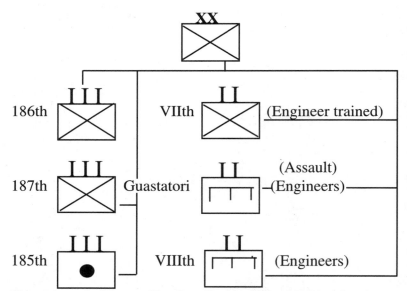

The Italian Folgore Parachute Division

186th — VIIth (Engineer trained)

187th — Guastatori — (Assault) (Engineers)

185th — VIIIth (Engineers)

This regiment had three artillery battalions made up of 47/32 anti-tank guns. They were the only ones which were air transportable, thus they were chosen for the regiment and used as "artillery."

BELOW: A New Zealand Army officer is photographed next to a Fiat CR42 fighter bomber, shot down near Buq Buq, Egypt.
- Author's Collection

ABOVE: The colourful tail insignia of the 150th Assault Squadron, which were equipped with Breda Ba65 ground attack aircraft. The squadron was operational in Libya from July to December, 1940.
- SA National Defence Force.

BELOW: The Caproni Ca310 light bomber. RIGHT: A damaged Caproni CA310 Libeccio; Often used as army co-operation aircraft. These mutli-role planes had steel tube fuselage covered with fabric and wooden wings!
- photgraph credit, ATL, Wellington, New Zealand

- line drawing, courtesy Antonio Munoz

ABOVE: An Australian officer stands next to a destroyed Savoia Marchetti SM79 bomber.

- Author's Collection

La Regia Aeronautica in North Africa

ABOVE, BELOW, & ABOVE RIGHT: The Italian Macchi MC200 fighter. It was nicknamed the "Saetta" (Thunderbolt). Maximum speed was 313 miles per hour at 13,760 feet. The range was 435 miles if the pilot kept an average speed of 280 miles per hour. The climbing speed was 3,100 feet per minute. The engine used was the 840 horse-power, 14 cylinder, air-cooled Fiat A74 RC38. Armament was two 12.7mm machine guns which were synchronized to avoid hitting the propeller of the airplane. The wing span was 34 feet, 8 inches, while the length of the plane was 26 feet, 10 inches. The plane was an all-metal construction and could hold a maximum of 163 gallons of fuel. Empty, it weighed 3,910 pounds while fully loaded the weight of the plane jumped to 5,440 pounds. The maximum serviceable ceiling of this fighter was 33,000 feet.

In the summer of 1942, the Italian 8th, 13th, and 150th Fighter Squadrons were still armed with this plane (while the 6th, 9th, 10th, and 17th Fighter Squadrons were supplied with the newer model MC202 fighter. One fighter group (the 3rd), was still equipped with the outdated CR42 bi-plane.

-Antonio Munoz Collection.

MALTA: THE INVASION THAT NEVER WAS

The invasion and ultimate capture of Malta from the British by the Axis never occurred, but had the plans gone through it is very likely that the Axis forces would have captured the island fortress and thus prevented the continued loss of men and material that the Malta based British naval and air forces were sinking on a monthly basis. Italian air force estimates as to the number of planes required for this projected invasion were as follows:

	German	Italian
Fighters	189	222
Bombers	216	270
Torpedo Bombers		36
Ground Attack Fighters	27	168
Transports	216	170
Gliders	27	
Rescue Planes	18	24
TOTAL:	693	890
GRAND TOTAL:	1,506	

The invasion never took place, and we can only speculate as to what might have been had the Axis successfully captured the island, but we know for certain that losses would have been great.

ABOVE: A little-known South African salvage and repair unit that repaired damaged captured German and Italian aircraft. The use of enemy equipment was a common occurrence in the North African campaign, especially when it was so difficult to bring in war material to the theater of operations. The Germans and Italians in particular, often sought out captured British (and later, American) hardware, out of pure necessity.
- SA National Museum of Military History

BELOW: British forces based on Malta meant that every Axis convoy route (pictured here by broken lines) were subject to attack by planes & ships based on Malta. The importance of this island is clearly seen by this map.

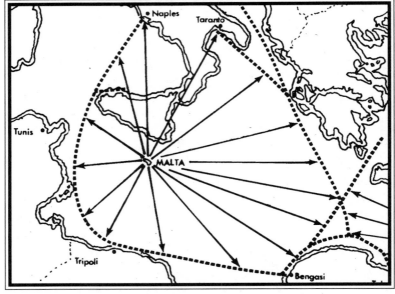

was decimated at El Alamein in late 1942. The survivors were reformed into the 285th Folgore Paratroop Battalion, which followed the fortunes of the Italo-German army and later fought in Tunisia.

Airborne trained Carabinieri formed the 1st Carabinieri Paratroop Battalion which was sent to North Africa in July 1941. However it soon suffered heavy combat losses and the survivors were eventually absorbed by the 285th battalion.

BLACKSHIRT DIVISIONS

The Blackshirts were in essence the armed force of the Fascist Party, although they were under the Royal Army's overall tactical control and were issued with army equipment and weapons (with the exception of the addition of Fascist insignia and dagger as a side arm). Six Blackshirt divisions were raised for service in the Ethiopian war in 1935. Another, the *7th Cirene*, was raised and deployed in Cirenaica as a precaution, should England enter the conflict. Besides training the *Cirene* sent a group of volunteers to each front in Ethiopia, while being engaged in fortification and road building in Cirenaica. It was demobilized in the summer of 1936, but later was resurrected with army personnel and called the 63rd (Royal) Infantry Division *Cirene.*

In September 1939 four blackshirt divisions were mobilized in Italy and shipped to Libya, they were renamed Libyan Blackshirt Divisions, these were the 1st *23 Marzo*, 2nd *28 Ottobre*, 3rd *21 April* and 4th *3 Gennaio*. In May, 1940 the *21 April* was disbanded and it's blackshirt personnel were used to strengthen the other blackshirt divisions. Its army personnel became part of the newly formed 64th Infantry Division *Catanzaro.*

ENGINEERS

The role of army engineers was mainly technical in nature, their asks involving mainly field work , construction, mine laying and removal. They had a good reputation for the quality of their road building and construction of fixed defences in Libya. Engineers were also responsible for all army signal communications. There were several combat battalions of elite assault engineers known as Guastatori who fought with distinction in North Africa, the 31st and 32nd Guastatori Battalions.

In August 1942 the 31st Battalion absorbed the 32nd after the 32nd was almost wiped out at Bir Matqua. The 31st went on to fight at El Alamein alongside the Folgore Parachute Division, but avoided destruction because it was motorized and managed to save itself during the retreat.

MILITARY POLICE

The military police or Royal Carabinieri were divided into two areas, Tripolitania and Cirenaica. Officers were seconded to each colony separately. The Carabinieri undertook general police duties within the colony, to checking and reporting on movements of all natives and foreigners, to escorting motor vehicles carrying mail or valuables, and to registering and controlling the movements of locals within their zones.

In time of war their duties included the supervision of traffic control, escorting of prisoners of war and the organization and administration of POW camps, the guarding of lines of communication and counter espionage. In the Tripolitania area the headquarters was in Tripoli and a division was allotted to the area. It had two companies at Tripoli, and one at Zuara, Garian, Misurata, Hon and Homs.

Companies were again divided into sub units called Tenenze which were commanded by a subaltern. The Tenenze were responsible for the Carabineri stations throughout the country. There was a station in every town and village of any size and at

110   continued on page 115

ABOVE: This interesting sign was attached to an upturned shovel in the region of the Tobruk front in mid-1941. It refers to a divisional section I, with the motto under the skull reading "without fear," while the name along the base mentions "the street of shifting shadows"- a probable reference to soldiers who have died in the war.

- Author's Collection.

RIGHT: An army engineer (left), with a comrade from the 69th Infantry Regiment of the 61st "Sirte" Infantry Division.
- Author's Collection.

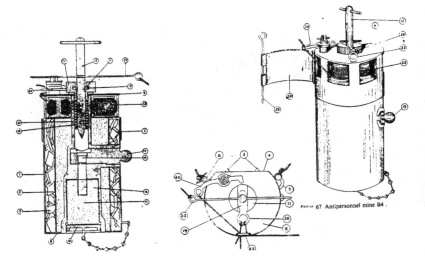

Figure 67 Antipersonnel mine B4 .

ABOVE & BELOW: The Italian B4 anti-personnel mine. These trip wire mines were used chiefly as a hindrance against moving targets' They had considerable effect blowing shrapnel over a radius of 10 meters. Photo taken around Tobruk, January 1941.

- ATL, Wellington, NZ

ABOVE & BELOW: The Italian B2 anti-tank mine. Here we see an Allied engineer disarming B2 anti-tank mines. These mines consisted of a welded metal box three feet six inches long with a metal lid which rested on two hinges. The lid had two openings covered by hinged flaps which corresponded to the position of the striker assembly and the wire-tensioning screw. It was 5 inches in breath and 4.7 inches in height. The filling was 3 kilos of TNT (about 7 pounds) in 200 gram blocks. The total weight of the mine was 33 pounds. The firing pressure was just under 100 kilos, which meant that anything weighing 220 pounds or more would ignite the mine.

- SA National Defence Force.

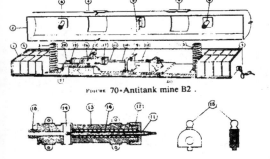

Figure 70 - Antitank mine B2 .

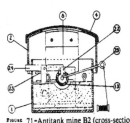

Figure 71 - Antitank mine B2 (cross-section) .

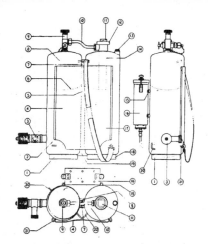

LEFT: The model 40 flame thrower
RIGHT: The model 35 flame thrower

BELOW: A British soldier test fires the Italian Model 40 flame thrower. These were issued to Italian assault pioneer units. They were rather heavy at 27 kilograms (59.4 pounds), with two cylinders containing nitrogen and fuel oil under pressure. The maximum range of the flame thrower was 16.5 meters with a maximum duration of 12 seconds.

- IWM.

114

certain points along the main roads. Tenenze in the larger villages had an establishment of 30 men and in the smaller 11.

In Cirenaica the headquarters was in Bengasi and an independent division was allotted to that area, with companies at Bengasi, Derna and Tobruch. The organization within the companies was smaller than that in Tripolitania. Carabiniere Gennaro Vetrano of the 339th Motorized Carabinieri section, 21st Army Corps relates:

"I volunteered for the Carabineri Corps on the July 1, 1939, I was 21 years old. My training was carried out in the Carabinieri school in Rome, where I obtained a motorcycle drivers license. I served in the Carabineri legion at Bari. It was while I was based in Bari that I got my orders to transfer to North Africa with the 339 motorized Carabinieri section of the 21 Army Corps.

"I left Bari harbour for Libya on May 30, 1940, on board the steamship Piemonte. All I knew about Libya was what I had learnt at school. When we disembarked at Bengasi in Cirenaica I was surprised to find that here was a pleasant city exactly the same as those found in Italy.

"On the June 4, I was embarked on the transport ship Livorno and was shipped to Tobruck. It was while stationed here I heard the news of Italy's entry into war.

"From Tobruck I was transferred to Bardia. During August there was a terrible explosion in one of the ammunition dumps and my commander, Second Lieutenant Greco, and other comrades were killed in the blast.

"From Bardia I took part in the advance to Sidi el Barrani in September 1940. I was attached to the command staff of the 21st Army Corp I came in contact with such people as General Bergonzoli and General Maletti.

"Of this period of my life I have very few pleasant memories, only the arrival of mail from home and riding along the coastal highway.

"I have many unpleasant memories: The hot Marmarica desert, the ghilbi wind that made you breath sand, the heat of the day and the cold of the night, the terrible bombardments from ships and aircraft.

"One night during December 1940 while I was sheltering in Field Hospital No.116 at Bardia, the order was given to retreat to avoid being encircled by the British. I was assigned to a convoy of three ambulances, on which was attached on each a big red cross flag.

"Our convoy headed off towards Tobruck. In the early evening between Bardia and Tobruck our column was machine-gunned by British tanks. I was in the last car. When I realized we were under attack I jumped out of the vehicle, what I saw was terrible. The first ambulance was on fire with bullets hitting the others. There was lots of screaming, many of the wounded were burnt in the vehicles.

"British duly arrived and picked up us few survivors. I was wounded during this attack. We were put in a captured Lancia 3RO truck. A British officer spoke to us. I could understand what he said, that, our Italian vehicles had the red crosses on the side but not on the front and as such the British did not see them.

"Soon after an Italian plane flew over the British column and I took the opportunity to escape. With me was an engineer soldier by the name of Giacomo Cassetta from Cavarzere and a Libyan corporal. We three got away and were eventually found exhausted by a column of mounted camel troops. We were taken to another hospital in the Tobruck zone."

MEDICAL CORPS

The army medical service operated under the umbrella of the North African Commissariat Corps. A wide range of medical facilities were available: Medical supply depots, field hospitals, convalescent hospitals, reserve hospitals, radiography facilities, dental surgeries and gas decontamination sections. These facilities were allocated to corps and divisions.

The medical section was an integral part of the divisional organization and had its own headquarters, vehicle unit and stretcher bearer detachment. The reputation of the Italian medical corps was high, it was the equal of any other army in North Africa.

Private Michele Figliola 21st Independent Medical Company recalls:

"I was conscripted when I was 20 years of age and did my initial training with the 7th Company Sanita of the 128th Regiment of the 41 Infantry Division Firenze at Florence, where I consider I received sufficient training.

"I was then transferred to the 7th medical company of the Pistoia Division, and from this 12 of us were sent on ahead to North Africa, to be joined by the main division later (though due to the fortunes of war we never did join up with them).

"Before I went to North Africa I knew nothing at all about it. I departed from Livorno for Libya by sea on July 18, 1942, In Libya I was initially shocked by the lack of greenery and all that sand. While I did not know any colonists personally I did visit them with soldier friends who had friends in these places.

"The uniform I was issued with was reasonably suitable and comfortable for the climate. Being medical personnel we were not supplied with much in the way of weapons. Just a rifle and an automatic pistol with several rounds of ammunition.

"I was attached to the 21 Autonomous Medical Company situated at Khalif Bomba about 13 kilometres from Benghazi until the retreat into Tunisia. I had little to do with the Germans - they appeared too arrogant, had too much in comparison to us and they flaunted it.

"During the retreat one night we camped in the desert, about 270 metres from the road, when we were attacked by British bombers. We were in a convoy of trucks, and when the planes

started to drop the bombs the soldiers scrambled from the trucks and away from the roadside. Some made it, others didn't. One scene in particular I vividly remember is that after the bombardment ceased we went to the aid of the others and one soldier appeared to be clinging upright to the side of one of the trucks, when we touched him, he fell down as he was dead.

"During the retreat while we were resting one time, British aircraft flew over and started firing at us. A sergeant major while answering the call of nature stood up and began to run with his trousers around his ankles. We all started to have a good laugh even though we were in a serious situation."

LEFT: A bomb disposal squad headed by a sergeant-major, kneel next to an unexploded bomb that fell close to the Red Cross First Aid clinic entrance of Tripoli hospital, late 1941.
- Author's Collections.

PART III
WAR IN THE DESERT
1940-1943

WAR IN THE DESERT

From the balcony of his office in Rome's Palazzo Venezia, Benito Mussolini announced to the large thronging crowd in the square below on June 10, 1940:

"Fighters of the land, the sea and the air, Blackshirts of the revolution and of the legions, men and women of Italy, of the Empire and of the Kingdom of Albania, listen! An hour marked by destiny is ringing in the sky of our country; the hour of irrevocable decisions.

"This declaration has already been given to the ambassadors of Great Britain and France. We are going to fight against the plutocratic democracy and reactionaries of the West that have always hindered the advance and endangered the existence of the Italian people..."

For all his rhetoric what Mussolini really wanted was a short war with little fighting. He was well aware of the weakened state of his armed forces and their inability to sustain an all-out war. Even with rearmament programmes under way, Mussolini stressed that it would not be until 1943 before Italy would be ready to join a conflict.

LEFT PAGE: An Italian soldier emerges from a dugout at Sidi el Barrani to brave the hot southern wind known as a "Ghilbi," which could blow for up to four days.

- James Burd

BELOW: A patrol of Saharina desert cars in southern Lybia. These very successful cars were used as reconnaissance vehicles to hunt and pursue the LRDG and SAS, as well as being used behind Allied lines. They had an operating radius of 800km cross country. The armament varied and could be 1 or 4 machine guns, a 13.2mm heavy MG, or even heavier armament such as a 20/65 AA gun, 20mm Soluthun anti-tank rifle, 37/45 or 47/32 anti-tank gun.

- James Burd

The "Saharina" patrol car, clearly ahead of its time in design, was exceptionally suited for desert warfare.

BELOW: A better view of the "Saharina" desert patrol car. It could clearly carry many jerry cans. This photo is of a Sahariani of the "Giovani Fascisti" (motorized) Regiment. It is armed with a 20mm AA gun.

- Antonio Munoz Collection.

However, he had difficulty aligning his political and military goals. He desperately wanted Italy to be seen as a strong ally to Germany by honouring the Pact of Steel, a military alliance between the two countries signed in early 1939. The stunning German victories in 1939 and 1940 convinced Mussolini that unless he acted soon there would be no honour or territorial gain for Italy.

King Vittorio Emanuele III was also concerned that if Italy entered the war too late there would be few spoils to be won. For although in private the king periodically complained about Mussolini when he felt he had encroached on his sovereign rights, in public at least he supported him. On June 10 Vittorio Emanuele signed Italy's declaration of war against the allies. The king issued a proclamation the following day:

"Soldiers of the land, sea and air!.

"As highest leader of all the forces of land, sea and air, following my feelings and the tradition of my house, like 25 years ago, I'm appealing to you all.

"I'm handing over to the head of the Government - Duce of Fascism, First Marshall of The Empire - the command of all the armed forces on all war theatres.

"My thoughts are with you while, like me loving our immortal country, you are allied with Germany, ready to face new challenges with unshakable trust and to overcome them.

"Soldiers of the land, sea and air!

"Knowing you as always, I'm sure that your valour and the patriotism of the Italian people will give victory to our glorious troops."

In mid-June Mussolini took a gamble and ordered Italian troops to advance into southeastern France on the heels of the German invasion. Such a last-minute undertaking resulted in little gain, at the cost of 631 dead and 2631 wounded.

The reward for this was the occupation of some French border towns and a demilitarization area along Italy's European and

BELOW: The officers of the 1st Battalion of the "Giovani Fascisti" Regiment (later, Division). They are seen here singing alongside their men. The officer in the middle of this picture is captain Baldassarri, who was called "PapaPallino" because of his kindly nature. The photo was taken in Gioda village, Libya on March 24th, 1942.

- Museum GGFF Ponti sul Mincio.

BOTTOM: Mortar crew of the "Giovani Fascisti" at Bir el Gobi, December, 1941.

- Antonio Munoz Collection.

North African borders with France. Mussolini had also cast his eyes on the rich prize of Egypt, just across the border from Libya. With Britain under constant bombing attack by the German Luftwaffe, he surmised it would only be a matter of time before it would be brought to its knees and occupied by the Germans.

With the announcement of war, a pessimistic Governor Italo Balbo made preparations as best he could for the defense of the colony, he knew there was a severe shortage of military material and in the preceding months had asked for reinforcements to be sent, but to no real avail. Balbo knew full well that any war in the Mediterranean would result in Libya being cut off from Italy, which would leave the budding colony in a perilous position both militarily and economically.

Libya and Italy were both dependent on the Mediterranean, but its two outlets to the ocean, were both controlled by the British. To the west was the straits of Gibraltar and to the east the Suez canal. Libya was to find itself at the declaration of war, sandwiched between two hostile neighbours, French Tunisia in the west and British occupied Egypt in the east. The need to defend two frontiers was a strain on it's already strapped resources. It was only after the signing of Italo-French armistice on June 24 that the threat from Tunisia was abated.

On June 28 while flying on an inspection tour of forward defenses in Cirenaica, Italo Balbo was accidentally shot down and killed by Italian anti-aircraft batteries at Tobruch, who mistook his aircraft for a British Bristol Blenheim bomber. Antonio D'Angelo of the 2nd Blackshirt Division 28 Ottobre Libica, recounted:

"When Balbo was killed, there were all sorts of rumours going around - that he was going over to the British side, that Mussolini had him killed, that he didn't know where he was going and lost course. None of this was ever proved and conspiracies always surface when an important leader

is killed in such a sudden and almost unbelievable way and history has proven this."

"Graziani had a special honour escort from each of the 4 Blackshirt Divisions (the Libica's 1st, 2nd, 3rd and 4th) sent to Tripoli to attend Balbo's funeral. I was part of this escort.

"I personally always admired Balbo's tenacity, his exploits, his Alpini service in WW1 and his fearless side. Also his masterful colonization of Libya - without any racist or prejudicial attitude towards the Libyans was well admired.

"He treated them at face value and elevated them in education and civilization.

"I was absolutely astounded at the funeral to see that the people who were wailing, crying and mourning the most were the Libyans, not the Italians"

"The Libyans kept saying 'Our Duce is dead, our Duce is dead, oh how could we have been so forsaken.' It was an incredible show of the love and devotion that the Libyan people had for Governor Balbo.

"When we saw this, everyone in my squad began to cry along with them, for a 'soldier' like Balbo, was, one of us, had truly been lost forever, and we didn't know what to expect in Libya after that." "Graziani was a great soldier, but he lacked the daring exploits of Balbo - one of the first Squadristi from Ferrara.

"Another thing I recall vividly was that it was so hot in Tripoli that I thought I was going to 'boil' in the sun. I remember some Libyans would 'cook' an egg right on the hood of a vehicle.!!"

With Balbo's tragic death, 58-year-old Rodolfo Graziani, Italy's foremost colonial officer, a Marshal of Italy and the Army Chief of Staff known as the "Lion of the Desert" was transferred to Libya as Governor and commander-in-chief. Graziani had orders to immediately advance into Egypt, but he refused to comply, instead demanding further reinforce ments of tanks, weap

continued on page 129

126

INSET: *Marshal Rodolfo Graziani, the Libyan theater com-*
mander who oversaw the initial, cautious Italian advance to
Sidi Barrani, Egypt in September 1940. In this earlier photo-
graph he wears the rank of General of an army corps. After the
disaster of Beda Fomm, he retired to private life.

- Author's Collection.

BELOW: *Chief of Staff in North Africa, General Curio Barbasetti di Prunn. He was a career artillery officer who replaced General Gambara in March, 1942 after Gambara was dismissed by General Cavallero.*

- Bundesarchiv Koblenz

ons and motor transport. For Graziani and his generals realised that without them only modest objectives could be achieved as motor transport counted for more than numerical superiority in men. As Italian Foreign Minister Count Galeazzo Ciano sardonically remarked:

"Never has a military operation been undertaken so much against the will of the commanders."

It was only after constant haranguing and the threat of dismissal from Mussolini, that the reluctant marshal, who had located his headquarters in an ancient underground Roman tomb at Cirene, ordered General Berti to advance the Italian ground force from his 10th Army across the Egyptian border.

The mass of infantry advanced on foot, infantry and anti-tank guns were lorry borne, while other artillery was motor drawn. Squadrons of medium and light tanks, along with artillery, screened the advancing infantry columns against attacks by marauding enemy mechanized units. The daily intelligence summary of the 10th Army for September 14, 1940 noted:

"...At 6am on the 13th after violent artillery
preparation against Musaid and Sollum, our troops crossed the frontier between Nizwet Ghirea and Sollum.
"At 6.30am our advance troops occupied Musaid.
"At 9am advanced patrols entered Sollum, which had been abandoned by the enemy and partly demolished.
"The advance continued all along the front and by evening some units had appeared on the Halfaya track.
"The enemy replied to our advance with occasional artillery action from the rear and by occasional aerial bombing. Enemy armoured cars and tanks kept at a distance from our troops, observing our movements and attacking here and there, but being repulsed by our anti-tank defences.
"Our losses. Some 40 killed and wounded. At 6am on the 14th, our advance was resumed along the front.

"The enemy replied with medium artillery between wadi Abbas and Alam El Kindad while armoured elements maintained contact. In the evening the enemy dropped bombs on Bambo and Menelao without causing damage.

"Deductions; During the past few days the enemy has carried out a policy of observation in the border strip, wearing tactics in the Buq buq area, and resistance in the Matruh area. In fact the enemy, in the face of an advance of men and material thought it prudent not to fight on the border and withdrew his infantry from contact, ordering mechanized units to maintain contact and delay the advance as much as possible.

"Our reports of September 2-13 indicated the border strip was less strongly held than before. It seems therefore that the enemy was at least partially surprised by our large use of mechanised units, anti-tank weapons and artillery and by the number of columns which crossed the frontier like an enormous avalanche. (The battle was concluded on the right wing after only four days).

"The enemy was therefore forced:

"1). To retire to strong positions suitably strengthened (distance and lack of resources are our enemies in the tactical supply field).

"2). To avoid excessive wearing of men and material now in order to conserve them for the time and place the British command select for battle. (probably Mersa Matruh).

The incursion had cost 120 Italian dead and 410 wounded. Orders were issued to construct a series of isolated fortified perimeter camps across 80km of desert from the coast near Sidi el Barrani inland. As the camps were considered only temporary staging points before the advance continued towards Mersa Matruh (with its railhead and airfields), the gaps between the camps were not fortified. Graziani said he needed to halt into order for his supplies to catch up. Not an easy task taking in consideration the general lack of motorized transport in some formations and the terrain.

Mussolini on October 28 launched an attack on Greece. This ill-advised military adventure was in part a reaction to the German occupation of Rumania and also a further step in Mussolini's ambitious plans for total Italian domination of the Mediterranean. The Greek campaign was to siphon off vital men and equipment needed in North Africa. The Italian Order of Battle for the ground forces in Libya and Egypt was the following in October 1940:

5TH Army: HQ Tripoli (General Italo Gariboldi)

10th Army Corp: Southwest of Tripoli, HQ at Garian (General Alberto Barbieri).

           25th Infantry Division Bolgona - semi-motorized. (General Mario Marghinotti).

           55th Infantry Division Savona (General Pietro Maggiani).

20th Army Corp: Troops southwest of Tripoli along the coast, but HQ was at Tagiura (General Ferdinando Cona).

           17th Infantry Division Pavia - semi motorized (General Pietro Zaglio).

           27th Division Brescia - semi motorized (General Giuseppe Cremascoli).

           60th Infantry Division Sabratha (General Guido Della Bona)

Headquarters High Command North Africa: HQ Cirene (Marshal Rodolfo Graziani).

21st Army Corp: HQ Beda Littoria (General Lorenzo Dalmazzo).

           61st Infantry Division Sirte - Beda Littoria (General Vincenzo Dalla Mura).

           2nd Blackshirt Division 28 Ottobre - Barta

(Luogotente General Francesco Argentino).

         Colonial Blackshirt Militia Volunteer Battalion - Barce.

Auxiliary units: 3rd Medium Tank Battalion (M13s arriving)
        Two paratrooper battalions - Tolemaide
        Superior command artillery
        20th Corps artillery - Bengasi
        10th Corps artillery - Soluch

10TH ARMY: HQ Bardia (General Mario Berti).
        Headquarters army troops and services.
        2nd Tank Group at Bardia (Colonel Antonio Trivioli). This consisted of one medium and one light tank battalion.
        1st Tank Group at Buq Buq (Colonel Pitassi Aresca). One medium and three light tank battalions.
        At Buq Buq was a frontier guard garrison under 10th Army control.
        A machinegun battalion of the Vittorio Emanuele II cavalry regiment.
        18th Libyan Battalion - Martuba.

22nd Army Corps: HQ Tobruch (General Pitassi Mannella)
        4th Blackshirt Division 3 Gennaio - El Adem
        (General Fabio Merzari)
        64th Cantanzaro Infantry Division - Gambut
        (General Lorenzo Mugnai).

23rd Army Corps: HQ Sollum (General Annibale Bergonzoli).
        62nd Marmarica Infantry Division - Sidi Omar - Halfaya Pass - Sollum and along escarpment. (General Ruggero Tracchia).

63rd Cirene Infantry Division - Rabit and Sofafi camps (General Alessandro De Guidi).

1st Blackshirt Division 23 Marzo - Between Buq Buq and Sidi el Barrani. Building roads, water pipeline and fortifications. (Console General Francesco Antonelli).

Libyan Divisional Group: HQ Sidi el Barrani (General Sebastiano Gallina)

1st Libyan Sibelle Division (General Giovanni Cerio)

2nd Libyan Pescatori Division (General Armando Pescatori)

Maletti Libyan Group (General Pietro Maletti)

A further factor which held up the continuance of the offensive from Sidi el Barrani against Egypt happened on November 11 when the British undertook an aerial torpedo attack on the Italian battle fleet lying in the harbour of Taranto, which resulted in the sinking of the dreadnought Cavour and serious damage to the battleships Littorio and Duilio. This neutralised the Italian battle fleet to such an extent that it allowed the British to operate a naval squadron (which included two aircraft carriers) in the region of Malta. In addition the RAF also flew from bases on Malta and southern Greece, harassing shipping between Italy and Libya and choking the flow of supplies to such an extent that a resumption of an attack was not considered at all viable at the time, although some authors contend that Italian supplies were diverted from North Africa in order to save the miliary situation in Greece. By November 25th / early December 1940 the Italian order of battle was:

10th ARMY

Sector Headquarters

I Sector (Sidi el Barrani): Commander General Gallina
        Headquarters Libyan Divisional Group:
        1st Libyan Division
        2nd Libyan Division
        1st Blackshirt Division 23 Marzo
        (began transferring to Bardia, December 1).
        4th Blackshirt Division 3 Gennio
        (began arriving from frontier, December 2)

II Sector (Buq Buq): Commander General Spatocco
        Headquarters 21st Army Corp
        Maletti Libyan Group
        63rd Cirene Division
        64th Catanzaro Division

III Sector (Sollum): Comander General Bergonzoli
        Headquarters 23rd Army Corp
        62nd Marmarica Division
        2nd Blackshirt Division 28 Ottobre

Under Marshal Graziani's direct orders
        Headquarters 22nd Army Corp.
        61st Sirte Division.
        Tank Brigade - General Babini
        Artillery of manoeuvre headquarters.
        60th Sabratha Division.

The layout of Nibeiwa camp was roughly rectangular and situated on a spur, covering approximately 2,194 meters by 1,645 meters. The perimeter consisted of a complete wall and sangars

continued on page 137

The Italian Armies at the Beginning of the North African Campaign

The Italian units in Libya were split up into two armies: the 5th in Tripolitania (western Libya), and the 10th in Cirenaica (eastern Libya).

Both armies had between them a total of five corps: Xth, XXth, XXIst, XXIInd, & XXIIIrd. The 5th Army began the war with the Xth, XXth, & XXIIIrd Corps, but after the French armistice, the XXIIIrd Corps remained in Tripolitania, while the other two corps (the Xth & XXth) were sent to Cirenaica. Its headquarters was located in Tripoli between 1939-1941, while in 1942 it was transferred to Firenze in Italy. The 5th Army began the war organized as follows:

Xth Corps: *"Bologna"*, *"Savona"*, and *"Sabratha"* Divisions.

XXth Corps: *"Brescia"*, *"Sirte"*, and *"Pavia"* Divisions.

XXIIIrd Corps: 1st *"Camicie Nere"*, 2nd *"Camicie Nere"*

the Italian 10th Army began the war having the following divisions:

XXIst Corps: *"Cirene"*, and *"Marmarica"* Divisions.

XXIInd Corps: *"Cantazaro"*, 4th *"Camicie Nere"*, & 1st Libica Division.

The 10 Army was brought up to the Egyptian frontier with its five Divisions and quickly strengthened from Tobruk and Bardia. Toward the end of August all the available tanks were gathered into two special groupings, of four battalions and under the direct control of the High Command in Libya (see- the Babini "Special Armored Brigade").

Also the two Libyan Divisions were set under one command, named the Libyan Group. Before the initial Italian offensive, 10. Army was organized as follows:

XXI Corps: Divisions *"Cirene"* and *"Marmarica"*

XXII Corps: Divisions *"Catanzaro"* and 4. *"Camicie Nere"*

XXIII Corps: 1. *"Camicie Nere"* Division and 202° Artillery Group; Garrison troops from Tobruk and Bardia.

The High Command ordered the Libyan Group (containing the 1st & 2nd Libyan Divisions) plus the "Sirte" Infantry Division to the southern regions of Cirenaica on the Egyptian frontier. Subsequently a new reorganization was brought about, in which the XXIst Corps, with the *"Sirte"* Division, and the *"28 Ottobre"* (Black Shirt) Division constituted the reserve; the XXIInd Corps remained unchanged, the XXIIIrd was reconstituted with the *"Cirene"*, *"Marmarica"*, and *"23 Marzo"* (Black Shirt) Division.

ABOVE: General Gastone Gambara (center) was General Ettore Bastico's Chief of Staff. General Bastico is pictured here on the right of the photo. Gambara previously held the same position with Rodolfo Graziani and Italo Balbo.

- Bundesarchiv, Koblenz.

NOTE: General Gambara and Bastico were both veterans of the Spanish Civil War.

LEFT: General Ettore Bastico, the "comandante superiore delle forze armate in Africa settentrionale" (Supreme Commander of the [Italian] Armed Forces in North Africa).
- Antonio Munoz Collection.

(stone emplacements above the ground), except for a small gap. Anti-tank obstacles were built on two faces 137 metres outside the perimeter, consisting of an artificial bank behind a shallow ditch. The bank was made by filling the space between the parallel walls of stone with sand from the ditch.

Nibeiwa contained more machinegun emplacements around the perimeter than any of the other camps. The defences of the other camps were similar to those of Nibeiwa, although Tummar West and Sidi el Barrani had barbed wire defences started. Inside the camps were medical posts, stores, mess rooms and sleeping quarters dug out of the ground with rock sangars around them and covered over with camouflage quarter shelters.

Facing the Italians were the 7th Armoured Division, 4th Indian Division and the 7th Royal Tank Regiment under the field command of General Richard O'Connor. The British plan of attack was for a brigade of the 4th Indian Division and the Matilda II tanks of the Tank Regiment take Nibeiwa during a short artillery bombardment. The force would then strike north and overrun the Tummar camps and Sidi el Barrani.

A small mixed force under Brigadier A. R. Selby from the Mersa Matruh garrison was to co-operate with the Indians and prevent the garrison at el-Maktila moving to the assistance of Tummar. The role of the 7th Armoured Division was to cover the deployment of the Indians. The Tank Regiment was assigned to protect the left flank and prevent an attack from the Sofafi area. The Royal Navy was to assist the Selby force by bombarding el-Maktila with the monitors Terror and Aphis and Sidi el Barrani with the monitor Ladybird.

At 7.35am on December 9 the tanks and supporting infantry attacked Nibeiwa, where they surprised a group of Italian M11 tanks from the Maletti motorized group warming their engines. These were soon overcome and destroyed. As the British tanks entered the camp the Italians gave them an extremely hot reception.

The Italian and Libyan infantry, initially caught unawares by the

British tanks, were horrified by the lack of effect their weapons had on the enemy armour. It was the same with the Italian gunners, who fought gallantly and fired accurately but were eventually over run.

It was similar at the Tummar camps, although the armour was not as strong with only a battalion of L3 tankettes being present. Again there was heavy fire against the British tanks. The Italian gunners fought well, supported by a tenacious defence by the men of the 2nd Libyan Division, but in the end the tanks had the same demoralising effect.

Sidi el Barrani also fell after the effective artillery fire of the Italian gunners was shattered. The garrison of the 4th 3 Gennaio Blackshirt Division was systematically pressed until its resistance finally collapsed.

Meanwhile the 1st Libyan Division had withdrawn from el-Maktila and was moving west along the coast to Sidi el Barrani, where it encountered British forces. Its artillery offered determined resistance before it was forced to surrender.

The following are excerpts from the war diary of Second Lieutenant Federico Gorio, of an artillery unit of the 1st Libyan division captured near Sidi el Barrani.

"1940

"16 Sept 15 minutes air raid.

"17 Sept Arriving at Sidi el Barrani.

"18 Sept Navy bombardment 0001 hrs.

"15 Oct Noon two aeroplanes flying very low. One of ours shot down by AA fire.

"16 Oct We leave Sidi el Barrani for el-Maktila.

"19 Oct We are awakened by the English artillery (3/4 of an hour firing) 0700 hrs. Our 105 guns answer.

"23 Oct From 7 to 10 last night heavy English firing. Fire ceased at 0005 hrs next morning. They retired, losing 2 men and maybe two prisoners. We captured two rifles and two machineguns.

"25 Oct Navy attack...Sandstorm.

"28 Oct Ultimatum to Greece.

"29 Oct No news here. These heroes with other's bravery have to fight elsewhere. Greece is fighting. "Poor Stooges".

"31 Oct 0730 hrs. Our artillery firing on enemy tanks.

"8 Nov 1730 hrs. 2 English guns fire 20-30 shots.

"12 Nov 0730 hrs. I'm leaving for Buq Buq. Hard work to be done.

"24 Nov Arrival of mines B2 for the defensive line of the division.

"25 Nov Morning we placed 36 mines. Afternoon 196 mines.

"26 Nov Whole day 186 mines.

"28 Nov 1300 hrs aircraft machineguns the division.

"29 Nov Found some English margarine which tastes very bad.

"30 Nov For the first time after two months I can read in bed with electric light.

"3 Dec Placed 36 mines.

"8 Dec Awaiting an enemy attack (Gurkhas). They are shelling Sidi el Barrani. The dance begins.

"9 Dec From 2310 to 2445 hrs. 3 units of navy are firing. 0700 hrs, revielle. Duel of land artillery till noon. 1230 hrs, air raid. Artillery firing still in progress. 1530 hrs, order to get ready to retire. 1630 hrs, fire ceases.

"10 Dec Leaving for el-Maktila at 0100 hrs. Arriving at Abiar el Drin at 0730 hrs. I work like a dog the whole day at H.Q. We fire at intervals. Nobody understands anything. 1700 hrs armoured cars attack. Two battalions (IX and X) surrender. Panic and general escape. We stop the Libyans and the lorries with revolvers in our hands. We stop the retreat. No sleep. Very cold. Down the line they're shooting during the whole night.

"11 Dec 0730 hrs English tanks break through - we are left nearly without artillery; the few pieces which are left (three

*105) are firing their last ammunition. With the last shot the
guns themselves explode. At C.K an English tank is trying to
capture the battery. Phone is calling us at H.Q. We go to
defend it, but we are forced to surrender with the majority
who have already done so. This is the end..."*

The 64th Catanzaro Infantry Division withdrew from its camp, as did
the 63rd Cirene Infantry Division, trekking westwards towards the
Halfaya-Sollum-Capuzzo line. The 63rd Cirene managed to escape
and link up with the 62nd Marmarica Infantry Division before moving across the frontier into Libya. The 64th Catanzaro was caught on
the coast road west of Buq Buq by the pursuing British.

A determined rearguard by Italian artillery covering the infantry retreat gave elements of the 7th Armoured Division a rough time before practically all of the 64th were forced to surrender.

Five days after the British counter offensive had begun General Berti
returned from Italy. He was, however, unable to cope with the rapidly deterorating situation and Graziani dismissed him.

The British victory at Sidi el Barani resulted in the destruction of
almost half the Italian forces assembled in Cirenaica for the invasion
of Egypt. By December 17 the remainder of the Italians in Egypt had
withdrawn across the border into Cirenaica and inside the fortified
perimeter of Bardia.

After the surprise attack at Sidi el Barrani, a pessimistic Graziani was
of the opinion Cirenaica could no longer be defended and that it
would be advisable to withdraw to Tripoli, putting the inhospitable
Sirte desert between his 10th army and the Army of the Nile.

But the high command told him to be more optimistic, so in light of
these orders he deployed the 10th army into three defensive groups,
at Bardia the 23rd Corps, at Tobruch 22nd Corps with

*RIGHT: The Italian defenses at Bardia. The Italians had placed strong
delaying positions astride the coastal road leading to and from Bardia.
In spite of this and the strong defenses in Tobruk, by the time of the
German arrival in North Africa, the Italians had lost Cirenaica (eastern Libya) and Tripolitania (western Libya) was being threatened.*

THE ITALIAN DEFENSES AT BARDIA

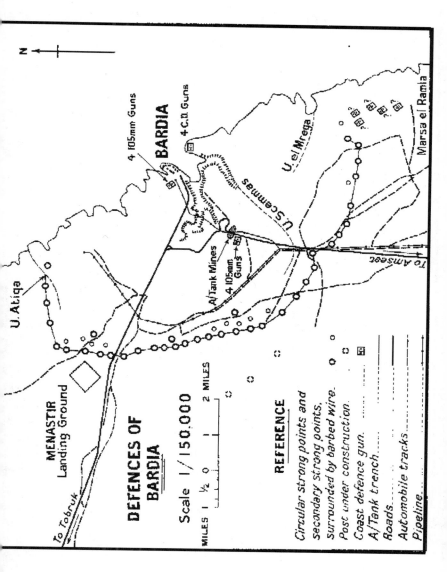

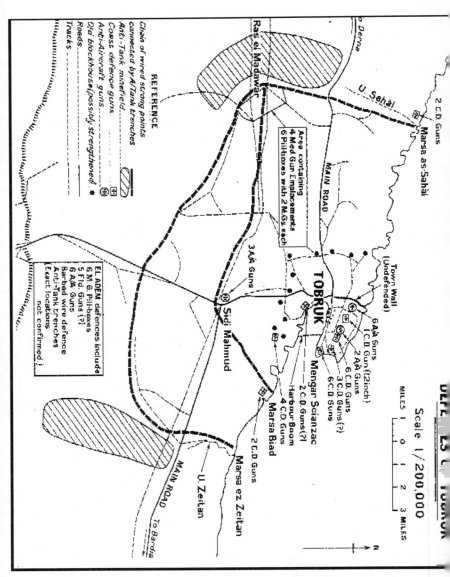

ABOVE: The elaborate defenses at Tobruk were not enough to prevent the port city's capture by the British army.

142

the 20th Corps holding the el Mechili-Derna line.

This bottling up of Italian forces left open the likelihood the defenders could be defeated piece-meal by an enemy greatly inferior in overall numbers. The force at Bardia under the command of General Annibale Bergonzoli comprised the headquarters and support troops of the 23rd Army Corps, in addition to the greater part of four infantry divisions.

The 62nd *Marmarica* was situated in the southern part of Bardia defences - 63rd *Cirene* also in the southern sector, 1st *23 Marzo* Blackshirts in the central sector, and the 2nd *28 Ottobre* in the northern part; corps troops with miscellaneous units, frontier guards and survivors of 64 *Catanzaro* Division in and around the port region. The whole force had an estimated strength of 26 coast defence guns, 290 field, medium and infantry guns, 146 anti-tank guns and 127 tanks (except for one company of M13/40s the majority of the armour was the light L3 tankette). Although many of the formations had been battered in the battle of Sidi el Barrani and morale was low, the Italians still possessed a field force capable - if given time to recover and reorganise - of being a threat to Egypt. Bardia itself was a small port 12km from the Egyptian border and the seaward anchor for the frontier wire. Its defences, prepared before the war began, comprised coastal and anti-aircraft defences and land mines, plus a fortified perimeter of 27km located mainly on the level plain south west of an escarpment falling to cliffs overlooking the Mediterranean.

The perimeter comprised a chain of concrete posts some 640 metres apart, each containing two or more medium machineguns and anti-tank guns, and surrounded by a circular anti-tank ditch and wire obstacle. The whole perimeter was protected by a continuous wire obstacle and much of it also by an anti-tank trench reinforced by mines. The forward posts were supported by another line 457 metres to the rear without anti-tank obstacles or continuous wire. The design of the forward and supporting posts was the same. Beyond the second chain of posts the main defences were battery positions and dugouts.

The British units used in the attack on Bardia were the 6th Australian Division (which replaced the 4th Indian Division now ordered to Eritrea in East Africa) and the 7th Royal Tank Regiment. The attack began at 5:30am January 3 and the battle raged until January 5, when the final pocket of Italian defenders surrendered in the southeastern sector. General Bergonzoli, managed to escape by foot across the desert to Tobruch.

16th Battery Sergeant Major Robert Donovan 2/2 Australian Field Regiment, Royal Australian Artillery, 6th Australian Division recalls:

"When we arrived in the Middle East, Italy had not entered the war, they were however still active in Abyssinia. We passed an Italian troopship in the Red Sea, quite close, there was an exchange of 'insults'. We thought badly of them, for what we perceived they were doing in Abyssinia.

"The following is not an example of gunners sticking together. The Italian artillery was definitely good at their trade. We occupied our position outside Bardia at night, a little after first light we got our baptism, accurate shell fire from their field guns. We were saved from serious casualties because of the amazingly poor quality of the projectiles, many failed to burst and those that did were ineffective. The gunners fought their guns to the last, many were found dead in their gun emplacements.

"At Bardia there were thousands of prisoners being moved to the rear. An Italian private soldier wandered into our vehicle dispersal area (wagon lines) and asked for water, the cooks obliged. He showed no desire to leave, so he was put to work, cleaning the cooking posts etc. He worked well and was quickly excepted by our troops, he did any tasks allotted, he had a good singing voice, he revealed that he was a diesel mechanic, and helped us get a couple of captured vehicles going, he was handy.

"No doubt he like us could hear the great number of Italian prisoners in a compound a couple of kilometers away, crying

144   continued on page 147

ABOVE: Two Bersaglieri (elite light infantrymen) relax outside their dugout at Bardia, sometime prior to the Allied attack on the port fortress.

- Peter Coleman

BELOW: Captured Allied soldiers are escorted from the battlefield by Italian guards. All captured enemy soldiers in North Africa were the responsibility of the Italians and were shipped to POW (Prisoner of War) camps in Italy.

- Rudy D'Angelo

ABOVE: An infantryman fires a bipod mounted Breda 6.5mm M30 light machine gun, while his crewman gives covering fire with an M91Carcano musket. Tobruk front, 11 November 1941.
- Authors Collection

'Aqua, Aqua' day and night, this no doubt gave him reason to stay with us, as we had plenty of food and water it was not a problem. He stayed until our move to Tobruch. I was then ordered to send him to the P.O.W compound. He was given food and water, and sent on his way, alone, crying, stopping every few yards, and shouting pleas to me to be allowed to stay. I felt lousy, but he went, I still wonder what happened to him."

The main Italian force now left in Cirenaica was at Tobruk, where the headquarters and support troops of the 22nd Army Corps were located along with the 61st *Sirte* Infantry Division, frontier guards, and the permanent coastal defence and anti-aircraft garrisons. Further west was the 60th *Sabratha* Infantry Division, while around the region of el Mechili the Italians were assembling an armoured formation. Ugo Tebaldini, artilleryman of the 61st Infantry Division Sirte relates:

"I was a conscripted into the artillery corps, where I was given able training. I felt we had a good relationship and understanding with our superiors.

"I sailed to Libya on the ship Argentina, where it landed on the Mediterranean coast at Homs, 120 kilometres east of Tripoli. All I knew about the colonies at that time was what I had learnt at school. We soldiers soon got on fine with our settlers, more so with the younger ones. We found the native Libyans to be good soldiers."

"I was chief of a gunnery battery in the Sirte Division. One night I misplaced a field gun, I finally found it after spending several hours searching for it, just in time to avoid being disciplined for losing it."

"About my views of Mussolini and the King one could write a book. We trusted them, but after some years of war we changed our minds. We then only had denigration and revulsion for both of them."

Tobruk had a good if small harbour, which was the only safe and accessible port for the 1600 kilometres, between Sfax in

Tunisia and Alexandria in Egypt. It had an adequate water supply, though not as good as that at Bardia, and had been developed as the main base for the Italian land and air forces in Cirenaica.

It was well protected by seaward and anti-aircraft defences and from land attack by a fortified perimeter of some 44km. The design and layout of the defences closely resembled those of Bardia. The exception was that the anti-tank ditch was in many places a bare 61cm deep and supplemented by mines defended by booby traps. The garrison, however, was weak in relation to the area it was required to defend.

Thousands of Italians tried to reach Tobruk after the defense of Bardia became hopeless and General Bergonzoli's party was one of those that made it to Tobruk. But Pitassi Mannella, Mussolini's 'great artillery general', was in command there and the 7th Armored Division had already cut the fortress off, so Bergonzoli was flown out to Derna, where he helped with the defenses there.

An attack on Tobruk was launched on January 21 by the 6th Australian Division and the remaining serviceable tanks of the 7th Royal Tank Regiment. In some sectors the Italians resisted strongly, but Tobruch fell on January 23, although not before the defenders had demolished installations and stores before surrendering.

Battery Sergeant Major Robert Donovan relates:

"After the first day of battle at Tobruk, we moved inside the Italian perimeter to prepare for the assualt on the inner perimeter around the town. This was done in pitch darkness on an Italian position, a few dug outs etc. Just before dawn the next morning I had a look around the area, saw some dead Italians, and suddenly ahead appeared from a dugout, a soldier wearing the Italian pith helmet, bearded and in an Italian uniform, he had a pistol in his holster. I drew my pistol and up went his hands. I noticed he was staring at my pistol and smiling, I looked down and saw I had left a piece of

continued on page 151

ABOVE: An 81/14 Model 35 mortar is loaded by its crew, Tobruch front, June 1941. This was the Italian version of the French 81mm mortar. In North Africa, the British took as many as they could find because they had better range than their 3 inch mortar. The 81mm had a range of 1,500 meters with a heavy bomb and 4,052 meters with a light bomb.

- Author's Collection

RIGHT: The 81/14 Model 35 mortar. The excellent design made it one of the best mortars of the war.

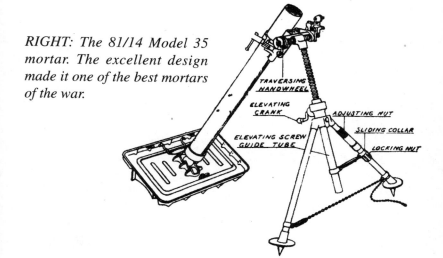

TRAVERSING
HANDWHEEL

ELEVATING
CRANK

ADJUSTING NUT

SLIDING COLLAR

ELEVATING SCREW
GUIDE TUBE

LOCKING NUT

ABOVE: General Ettore Manca di Mores (right) in conversation with Colonel Griccioli (left) and two subalterns, Tobruk, June-July 1941.
BELOW: General Bartolo Zambon, of the "Brescia" Infantry Division, during the siege of Tobruk, May-June 1941.

- Franco Festa Archives.

cleaning cloth in the muzzle to keep the sand out. We both started to laugh, I took his pistol, told him to sit down and empty his pockets, he showed me a photo of his wife and two kids. He was older than me, in his mid thirties I guessed. I was 22. We talked, with difficulty, some sign language, a nice man, we gave him some breakfast, and sent him on his way with an escort. We shook hands.

"An Italian artillery Captain, was handed over to me to move him to the rear. He spoke good English, a very courteous man, while we waited for a vehicle to move him, we talked about the war and fascism. He was a journalist in Italy, and said if you wanted to exist in Italy you had to join the party. He was worried about how he would be treated as a P.O.W. I assured him his treatment would be humane. I saluted him when he left, he was surprised, returned the salute and we shook hands. I found the Italians that I met to be ordinary men doing a job that they did not enjoy."

General Ferdinando Cona was in overall charge of the Derna defensive area with the 20th Army Corps and had orders to block the two main approaches to Bengasi. The northern line of advance through Derna was covered by an ad-hoc formation of 5000 men from different units under the command of General Bergonzoli. These consisted of metropolitan infantry, Libyan infantry and paratroopers, Bersaglieri, a platoon of M11 tanks and some armoured cars. In the sector of Berta-el Mechili was a force of 14,000 men from the Sabratha Division, the Babini armoured brigade and minor units.

The Babini brigade had 57 M13 medium tanks and 25 light tanks. Between Derna and el-Mechili rose the jagged hills of Gebel el Achdar which reached a height of 502 metres. The Gebel was a barrier to attacking mechanised forces, but also had the effect of cutting off the defenders of Derna from the armour at el-Mechili, which meant the formations were forced to fight independently of each other.

On January 24 the 6th Australian Division advanced towards

Derna, while the 7th Armored division fell on the Babini Brigade. The defenders of Derna put up dogged resistance against the attacking Australian infantry, making them pay for every centimetre of earth in a series of savage rearguard actions. It was the most fierce resistance yet encountered by the allied troops. The Babini Brigade withdrew into the Gebel el Achdar to avoid encirclement. But in doing so they gave the British a clear road to the main Italian supply line along the Gulf of Sirte, which would have left all the Italian forces in the Gebel bottled up.

From February 3 General Tellera was given command of all the troops in Cirenaica. Graziani went to Tripolitania to oversee the new operative phase and Tellera put General Cona in charge of the withdrawal of troops from the Gebel into Sirte. He had under his command three motorized columns headed by Generals Della Bona, Bergonzoli and Villanis. The distance between el Mechili and Beda Fomm across country was about 225 kilometres. Along the coast road between Derna and Beda Fomm it was about 362 kilometres. The retreating Italians had the advantage of using the Via Balbia, while the British had to contend with a poor reconnoitred track which crossed a desert consisting of either soft sand or areas strewn with large rocks.

At noon on February 6 elements of the 7th Armoured division reached their objective at Beda Fomm just half an hour before the first Italian column headed by General Della Bona, which was streaming westwards from Bengasi down the Via Balbia. The Italians were not expecting to be attacked so far from the front lines and were not prepared for quick action, with inadequate flank or rearguard protection.

Throughout the day the British force checked and shelled columns of transport consisting of infantry in lorries, artillery and tanks, as well as rear echelon personnel, colonial administrators and frightened civilians. These non-combatants sought to surrender as soon as they could. During this grim action the Italians hit out wildly as they came up against the British blocking their retreat. Many Italian tanks were destroyed, though they fought with desperate determination, as did the supporting infantry and artillery. They were in a hopeless situation, pinned to the road in long, unmanageable columns of vehicles extending back almost 32km, the clash was fought in an area between the 70km and 30km milestones on the Via Balbia.

The next day after a dawn attack by a scratch force of Italians failed, the heart went out the resistance and soon the battered survivors lay down their arms. General Tellera had been mortally wounded during a tank battle and died a few hours later. The HQ of the 10th Army, as well as Generals Cona, Babini and Bergonzoli, were also captured. In four pitched battles General O'Connor had advanced 901 km from his starting position. Although there were never more than two divisions under his command, he had destroyed the Italian 10th Army which resulted in 130,000 men being taken prisoner - including 22 generals and an admiral, 380 tanks and 845 artillery pieces captured or destroyed.

The main British advance continued along the coast to el Agheila at the bottom of Gulf of Sirte. This was an important position for there was only a narrow gap about 24-32 km wide through which tanks could pass between the desert and the sea. In this position the British XIII Corps was in a good location to invade Tripolitania or defend Cirenaica as required.

From el Agheila British patrols ventured into Tripolitania before Commander-in-Chief Middle East, General Archibald Wavell , reined in General O'Connor who, having signalled "one fox killed in the open", was already looking ahead to another, the Italian 5th Army defending Tripoli. Wavell, however, wanted to conserve his remaining forces in the desert so he could concentrate on Churchill's Greek adventure.

This was a major blunder on the allied side as there were few strong formations left in Tripolitania to oppose them in early 1941. The occupation of Tripoli at that time would have pre-

Continued on page 157

ABOVE: A sea of dejected Italian prisoners huddle together in the open desert after their capture during the British operation against Sidi el Barrani in December, 1940

- Domenico Sansotta

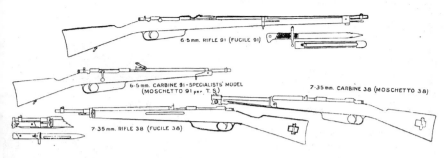

ABOVE: Some basic Italian army rifles and carbines. From top to bottom, the 6.5mm Rifle 91; The 6.5mm Carbine 91 Specialists' model; The 7.35mm Carbine 38 (Moschetto 38); And the 7.35mm Rifle 38 (Fucile 38).

BELOW: A soldier inspects a Carcano 6.5mm rifle, from a large stockpile of Italian rifles captured during the early Allied push through Cirenaica.

- ATL, Wellington, NZ

RIGHT: General Federico Ferrari Orsi, the commander of the Xth Corps.

Xth Corps

February 1941-
"Pavia" Infantry Division
"Bologna" Infantry Division
"Ariete" Armored Division
(9,000 men; 117 light tanks, 46 medium tanks, 97 artillery pieces).
5th (German) Light Division
(7,000 men; 27 armored cars, 55 light tanks; 130 medium tanks; 111 artillery pieces).

January 1942-
"Brescia" Infantry Division
"Pavia" Infantry Division

May 1942-
"Brescia" Infantry Division
"Pavia" Infantry Division

July 1942-
Between the Xth and XXIst Corps, these two Italian corps could only muster at this time, eleven battalions of infantry, with an average of 200 men per battalion. Between them, they had perhaps 30 heavy artillery batteries, and 11 light artillery batteries.

September 1942-
[At the battle of Alam el Halfa - 15,800 men]
"Brescia" Infantry Division (4,300 men)
"Folgore" Parachute Infantry Division (5,200 men)
"Ramcke" (German) Parachute Brigade (4,000 men)
Xth Corps Troops (2,300 men)

23rd October, 1942-
"Brescia" Infantry Division
"Pavia" Infantry Division

vented future axis build up and finished the North African campaign there and then.

The Allied advance through Cirenaica had by passed the isolated garrison fort of Giarabub deep in the desert some 240km south of Bardia on the Libyan border. It consisted of 2000 Italian and Libyan soldiers under the command of Colonel Costiana. A force consisting of the 6th Australian Divisional Cavalry and support elements including the LRDG were sent to observe it and to prevent supplies reaching it in the hope the troops would starve and surrender.

Even though the defenders' daily rations were dropped to a biscuit and a small tin of meat per man - and almost all the Libyan troops deserted - the garrison still held out. On March 21, 1941, the Australian led force assaulted the fort during a sand storm, and it fell after sharp skirmishes. An estimated 1300 officers and men were captured, some wounded, while 250 men were killed and 36 guns of various calibres taken. Lance Corporal Mick Allen, Medical Orderly, Long Range Desert Group, R Patrol, relates his part in the siege of Giarabub:

"We, R Patrol, left the Citadel, Cairo, on New Year's Day, 1941, proceeded to Dalla, crossed the Sand Sea and joined some Australian troops (including the Australian Div Cav) to assist them in the siege of the Giarabub fortress. Our particular task was to prevent any supplies from reaching the garrison and to preventing anybody from leaving. An artillery troop of four guns (25 pounders) fired 12,000 rounds into Giarabub. The troop commander had received instructions to avoid damaging the mosque and it is to the credit of the gunners that only one shell passed through the dome.

"We heard an Italian convoy was coming from the direction of Derna and we were told to get at it. Now, whenever aircraft passed overhead, we had no system of recognition and whether the aircraft was enemy or not, we had to go to ground and wait until all was clear. While we were heading for this enemy convoy, the RAF came on the scene and attacked our target. When

XXth Corps*

*[Initially known as the *"Corpo Di Manovra,"* or Maneuver Corps]

17th November, 1941-
A) 132nd "Ariete" Armored Division.
B) 101st "Trieste" Motorized Infantry Division.
C) Reconnaissance Group (containing the following units):
1st Group "Giovani Fascisti" (two motorized Blackshirt infantry battalions); One battalion, PAI (Polizia Africa Italiana, or Italian African Police) "R Gesi" [two motorcycle and one armored car company]; LIInd Tank Battalion (M 13 tanks); III/32 Tank Battalion (L-3 tanks); One mixed armored car and L-3 tankette company; Two artillery battalions (65/17 guns); 13th Independent Artillery Company (100/17 guns); 14th Independent AA Company (20mm guns); 11th Independent Artillery Company (65/17).

January, 1942-
"Ariete" Armored Division
"Trieste" Motorized Division

July, 1942-
The entire "corps" could only muster 1,600 riflemen in 8 weak battalions, 54 tanks, 40 (heavy) anti-tank guns, and 6 light artillery batteries.

September, 1942-
[At the battle of Alam el Halfa- 18,600 men]
132nd "Ariete" Armored Division (7,200 men; 50 armored cars; 126 tanks and self propelled guns)
"Littorio" Armored Division (4,600 men)
"Trieste" Motorized Infantry Division (5,300 men)
XXth Corps Troops (1,500 men)

23rd October, 1942-
132nd "Ariete" Armored Division
"Trieste" Motorized Infantry Division

RIGHT: General Giuseppe De Stefanis, the commander of the XXth Corps.

BELOW: Schematic diagram of the principal combat units under the *"Corpo Di Manovra"* (Maneuver Corps), the precurser of the XXth (Mechanized) Corps; As it appeared on 17th November, 1941:

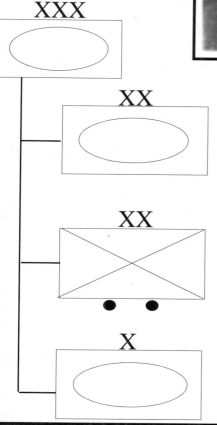

132. divisione corazzata "Ariete"- Gen. M. Balotta

101.divisione della fanteria motorizzata "Trieste"- Gen. A. Piazzoni

Raggruppamento esplorante- Colonel De Meo

eventually we were able to get there, we found they had hit vehicles containing ammunition and petrol. There were eight diesel tractors and about twice as many trailers. Among the cargo we found lemons, tea, bully beef, biscuits and many barrels of cognac, all of which had been abandoned by the Italians. We destroyed what we could and mined the road. Some time later a Lancia truck struck a mine and, although it was not greatly damaged, the driver must have jumped on to another mine which blew him to pieces. We took the Lancia to Siwa...

"Before Giarabub fell we endeavoured to assist an Australian manoeuvre by demonstrating to draw the enemy's fire from the fortress, which would not only distract his attention but would waste his ammunition. The first salvo passed beyond us, but the second fell right among our vehicles. We had no weapons with which we could get within reach of the enemy, but while we waited for a signal from the Australians we stayed in the same position. When we discovered the Australians were making a hasty withdrawal, however, we decided that was good enough for us and pulled out very smartly. A shell landed in one position immediately our trucks left it.

"When Giarabub fell, we found hundreds of rounds of ammunition and large quantities of food concealed under the mosque which our artillery had avoided so carefully. We also found two dead Italians in the well from which British troops were drawing water.

"We returned to the abandoned Italian convoy to salvage six of the eight diesel tractors. These were splendid vehicles, the most up-to-date American model. They had USA emblazoned on them...Each weighed between 12 and 14 tonnes. I think this was the largest enemy convoy that ever fell into the hands of the LRDG.

"We spent 13 weeks at Giarabub, although it had been intended we should stay there for three weeks. Towards the end of the siege we wore out our boots, socks and shirts. We were fed by the Australians. During the whole time we had only one wash,

RIGHT: General Enea Navarini, the commander of the XXIst Corps.

XXIst Corps

10th September, 1941-
17th "Pavia" Infantry Division
25th "Bologna" Infantry Division
27th "Brescia" Infantry Division
"Sabratha" Infantry Division*
*(shared with another corps)

17th November, 1941-
17th "Pavia" Infantry Division
25th "Bologna" Infantry Division
27th "Brescia" Infantry Division
102nd "Trento" Motorized Infantry Division
XXIst Corps Troops: 3rd, 5th, 8th, 16th, & 24th Artillery Regiment; 340th Frontier Guard Artillery regiment, XXXIst Guastatori Battalion.

January, 1942-
"Sabratha," "Pavia," and "Trento" Motorized Infantry Divisions.

May, 1942-
"Sabratha," & "Trento" Motorized Infantry Divisions; 90th (German) Light "Africa" Motorized Division.

8th July, 1942-
Between the Xth and XXIst Corps, these two Italian corps could only muster at this time, eleven battalions of infantry, with an average of 200 men per battalion. Between them, they had perhaps 30 heavy artillery batteries, and 11 light artillery batteries.

September, 1942- [during the battle of Alam el Halfa]
"Trento" Motorized Infantry Division (5,200 men)
"Bologna" Motorized Infantry Division (4,800 men)
164th (German) Infantry Division (10,600 men)
XXIst Corps Troops (3,700 men)
[In October, 1942 the corps had the same units, minus the 164th Division]

THE BABINI BRIGADE:
HOW A FEW ITALIAN TANKS, BACKED UP BY SOME GUTS, PREVENTED A COMPLETE COLLAPSE OF ITALIAN FORCES ON THE CIRENAICA FRONT

In 1941, the 10th Army was severely mauled by the English in Cirenaica; First at Beda Fomm (February 5th, 1941), and then at Benghasi (February 6th), where 80 Italian tanks were destroyed and 7 generals captured (including General Bergonzoli)! Worse still was the surrender of 20,000 Italian soldiers, 200 artillery pieces and 120 tanks captured by the British at Beda Fomm on February 7th, 1941.

There were some actions during those bleak winter months, which prevented a total collapse of the Italian front in Cirenaica. One such incident happened on December 9th, 1940 when the Italian Tummar posts destroyed 14 British tanks and the "Maletti Group" managed to knock out 35 out of 57 Matilda tanks using M 11 tanks! General Valentino Babini (who at one time led the "Sirte" Division), employed the newly created *"Brigata Corazzato Speciale"* (Special Armored Brigade), destroying or disabling 21 enemy tanks out of a Britsih force of 177 tanks and other armored vehicles on January 24th, 1941. His brigade's feat temporarily halted the British drive. These actions, and others like them, helped to keep the Italian front from collapsing altogether.

Since the start of the British offensive three months earlier, Italian losses had included 20,000 killed, 120,000 captured, and the loss by destruction or capture of 850 artillery pieces and 400 tanks. In effect, the Italian 10th Army had been destroyed. On February 12th General Erwin Rommel and the advance units of the Afrika Korps arrived in Tripoli. The Italian 10th Army was reconstituted and a new round of battles began.

when we were able to make a short visit to Siwa."

O'Connor's exhausted veterans were replaced with fresh but green troops. The 6th Australian Division was stood down as it was being sent to Greece and was replaced by the 9th Australian Division. The greatly-depleted 7th Armoured Division returned to Egypt to rest and refit, being replaced by half of the 2nd Armoured, two of whose regiments had to be equipped with captured Italian M13 tanks.

This lull in the British offensive gave the Italians a respite and time to reorganise. For although Beda Fomm was a severe setback 7000 Italians and 1300 Libyans managed to escape into Tripolitania. The Sabratha Infantry Division was reformed almost immediately from this pool with the addition of reinforcements from Italy. After Beda Fomm Marshal Graziani retired to private life. Mussolini convened a board of inquiry headed by Grand Admiral Paolo Thaon di Revel whose findings were critical of Graziani, but no action was taken against him. Sixty two-year-old General Italo Gariboldi, previously the commander of the 5th Army in Tripolitania, was appointed his replacement on February 11, 1941.

NAVAL CONVOYS

The primary operational goals of the Italian Navy at the beginning of the war were the defence of the central Mediterranean and to keep open the sea route to Libya.

The navy adopted a policy of tactical defence, as it reasoned was less risky than offensive operations with its inherent risk of losses, it felt it could not afford. However, through an incredible blunder by Mussolini merchant vessels overseas were not warned in time to return to Italy before war was declared, and 212 ships were lost without a shot being fired, totalling 1,236,160 tonnes. This left 604 serviceable ships with a total gross tonnage of 1,984,292 tonnes at the beginning of hostilities (including 56 German cargo ships stranded in the Mediterranean). Convoys were the main means of transporting vital war material and reinforcements to the beleaguered colony.

ABOVE: Ships at anchor in an Italian harbor (most probably Naples). Note the dazzle camouflage paint on the freighters.

- Dal McGuirk

Although supplies were desperately needed the convoys were not large because of a number of factors: The relatively short sea route between Italy and North Africa, and the inadequate berthing capacity of Libyan ports, which allowed only a small number of ships to be off-loaded at one time. Mussolini had earlier rejected a proposal that the ports of Tripoli and Bengasi be modernised

There was a shortage of auxiliary vessels, and the dearth of escort vessels meant convoys had to be proportional to the cover that could be provided. The escorts consisted of overworked torpedo boats and destroyers. Apart from a few armed merchant cruisers the navy had not created an auxiliary fleet. Sergeant-Major Luigi Bonechi of the 2nd Group 75/27, 36 Artillery Regiment of the Forli Infantry Division, recounts:

"During the summer of 1942 I was stationed in Greece with my division at Pireo Harbour, Athens."

"I volunteered as a gunnery specialist on a armed merchant freighter called Bucintoro [1,273 tons] which had been shipping coal to Mersa Matruh in Egypt.

"While on board I was under naval command and was in charge of several Breda 20mm cannons for anti-aircraft defence. These proved invaluable as we were attacked twice on the voyage, first by a Sunderland flying boat and then by an American plane. Luckily, however, we managed to arrive at our destination in one piece."

Additionally, the Italians suffered from a shortage of fuel oil which limited many operations - a serious ongoing problem never fully resolved. For example, in 1941 the navy required 101,604 tonnes of fuel oil monthly but received only 45,722 tonnes. The Germans were at that time sending seven fuel trains to Italy a day, but it was not enough to cover the deficit. Convoys bound for Libya were exposed to constant attack. They were initially set upon by submarines ranging off the Italian coast.

ABOVE: A Mediterranean crossing.

- Dal McGuirk.

CENTER & BELOW: The Italian destroyer "Dardo."

- Author's Collection.

Then further out were airborne onslaughts by radar-equipped aircraft (after mid-1941), attacks by roving submarines and the risk of surface raids by British Royal Navy vessels from Malta. Closer to the Libyan coast were more patrolling submarines and aircraft, and when the ships reached port there was still the ever-present danger of being bombed ore shelled at their moorings.

A British propaganda radio broadcast in September 1942 recounted to its listeners an attack by a British bomber, captained by a New Zealand flight sergeant on an axis freighter bound for Tobruch:

"Out of Genoa under a full head of steam an Axis freighter cleaves the rolling Mediterranean swell. Her bows point southwards towards Tobruch. She is carrying supplies for Rommel's garrison, for this is a night in September 1942....
She is a sizeable vessel of some 6,096 tons and capable of a good turn of speed. Laden to her mast she carries a cargo of fuel for tanks in drums and barrels, ammunition, food, guns and stores...
"She is a valuable ship to the enemy, this one that beats through the Mediterranean night. Just how much store is placed on the arrival of her cargo at Tobruch can be judged from the fact that she travels with an escort of eight destroyers. It is a desperate mission in a desperate cause on which she is engaged. Her engines have been running on full ahead for hours now and her heavy stem crashes against the surge of the sea as she drives southward.
"This ship will not reach Tobruch. Her fate is already been decided. Information of her whereabouts has reached Air Headquarters at Alexandria and even now a British torpedo bomber is on its way with orders to sink her. Going up the coast to raid Tobruch and shipping in the harbour is a squadron of British bombers. A radio message to the leader of the formation gives him the approximate position of the enemy

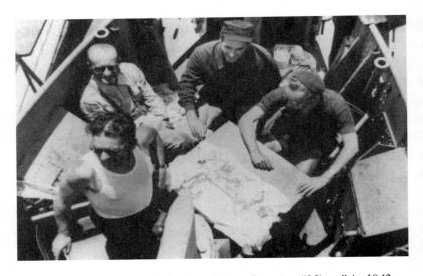

ABOVE: Officers on the bridge of the submarine "Micca" in 1942, during a transport run to Libya.

- Achille Rastelli.

BELOW: Two Italian freighters lay at anchor in the bay at Bardia, Cirenaica, 1940.

- Author's Collection.

freighter and he receives orders to send one of his machines after the merchantman.

"Not yet aware the air force has got her number, the Axis freighter is making all possible speed. Ahead and on either side of her the escorting destroyers keep watch. Their orders are clear. They must fight the merchantman way through to Tobruch at all costs. The greater part of the journey is safely over, but now with the goal only a few hours steam away, every revolution of the screw brings danger ever nearer.

"The bright moonlight gives them good visibility. The men at their watching stations are tense and alert. They expect the hand of Britain to strike but they repeatedly ask themselves will it strike from the air or from beneath the surface of the sea. British bombers and submarines deny all Axis ships safe passage in these waters.

"Axis seaman must keep watch for both. On board the merchantman the crew to a man know their ship has now entered a zone that had become the graveyard of many sisters British torpedoes have sent plunging to the bottom on just such a mission as this. The drone of powerful engines heard faintly in the distant sky brings every gunner to his post. This is it. As yet the adversaries have not sighted each other, but it will not be long.

"Flying high for better reconnaissance the British bomber crew takes full advantage of the bright moon to scan the spaces of the Mediterranean. To take a general look at the position before going in to the attack the New Zealander at the controls makes a wide sweep round the merchantman and her escort. Things look very businesslike on those eight destroyers below. No chance of surprise here. Those guns are quite ready to throw a lethal shower of flak into the air.

"All guns on the eight destroyers burn vivid flashes into the night throwing up a barrage intended to deny the bomber passage. The first run in by the bomber is a dummy. The pilot does not want the freighter's captain to from which angle he *intends to launch his torpedoes from...*

"Now comes the bomber's real attack. Down on the port quarter the pilot takes his machine, skimming the waves at a height of less than ten feet. At this angle he is not an easy target for gunners on the enemy ships, who are working strenuously to bring all possible fire to bear on the madcap New Zealander defying them. Close in he presses his attack. The range now so short that a miss is impossible...

"The aim is cool and deadly. Seconds later comes a muffled roar and a brilliant flash of light as both torpedoes strike the freighter amidships. The impact and explosion heel her over. Quickly a red glow spreads over her. She goes on fire fore and aft and begins to sink. Men rush to her sides and go over board into the sea.

"The bomber suffers too. As the aircraft turns away after delivering the freighter its death blow a shell from the guns of one of the destroyers spurts under her starboard engine.

The fuselage is blown in and the radio operator is wounded.... Another shell burst just below the aircraft tears away the port a landing wheel. Speed quickly puts the bomber once more out of range. Axis naval men cease fire and set about picking up survivors from the crew of the freighter now going down stern first to her grave."

The British ability to intercept at will almost any Italian supply convoy sailing to North Africa was attributable to a top secret intercept programme code named ULTRA which allowed them to read Italian and German cyphers passing between Rome and Berlin and the Axis armies in Africa. Without adequate supplies, the Italo-German armies were unable to put up any sustained resistance to the British after El Alamein.

Malta was the thorn in the side of Italy's operational freedom and its elimination as a British naval and air base became imperative.

Immediately on Italy's declaration of war, the Italian air attack on Malta began; an attack that was to ebb and flow for three

CONVOY DEFENSE:
ITALIAN SURFACE VESSELS

The problem of supplying the Axis forces in North Africa was a difficult one, given the fact that the British air and naval forces had access to the Italian & German supply routes and therefore were capable of attacking the Axis life line at will. The Regia Marina did its best to try and escort their merchant marine ships to and from the North African coast and back to Italy. Here is a brief look at their primary surface ships by class:

ABOVE: Destroyer Escort, Partenope Class. Length was 267 feet, with a displacement of 1,200 tons and a speed of around 27 knots. These vessels were basically oversized torpedo boats that were ideal for convoys and made excellent replacements when destroyers were not available or on short supply. They were very lightly armed but could provide some sort of anti-submarine protection. If they were faced with anything larger than themselves, they were almost certainly destroyed, and accounted for 20% of all Regia Marina losses during the war (41 such vessels).

ABOVE: Destroyer, Aviere Class. Length was 350 feet, with a displacement of 2,400 tons and a speed of 38 knots. While the ships of this class which the Regia Marina possessed at the outbreak of war were relatively modern, they had apparently been designed for employment at relatively close distances from their bases (i.e.- they were suited for the Mediterranean, but not for use in the Atlantic). It was thus that they tended to be outclassed by their British counterparts who were created for employment far from English shores. Forty-four destroyers of this class were destroyed during the war and amounted to 24% of Italian naval losses.

ABOVE: Cruiser Escort, Capitani Romano Class. Length was 465 feet, with a displacement of 5,420 tons and a speed of 40 knots. These ships were specifically designed for convoy escort and were hailed as a success. They were fast and maneuverable, all extremely important elements when fighting submarines. The one drawback to these ships was that of the 12 CE's which the Regia Marina planned to employ, only four were ever produced (and one of these was completed after the end of the war). Their small quantities thus limited their use.

ABOVE: Light Cruiser, Montecuccoli Class. Length was 598 feet, with a displacement of 8,990 tons and a speed of 37 knots. Of the twelve light cruisers built by the Regia Marina and employed during the war, six were destroyed. The twelve were divided into the "Condottieri" and "Montecuccoli" classes, but were basically the same design, with a variance in the displacement in tonnage of between 7-12,000 tons, the difference being made up for in slightly faster speed and better armor protection. The Allies considered this crusier design to be very successful.

ABOVE: Heavy Cruiser, Zara Class. Length was 600 feet with a displacement of 14,500 tons and a speed of 33 knots. This heavy cruiser style, of which there were four out of Italy's seven heavy cruiser fleet, was the average model. These vessels were well armed and well protected but could not be expected to stand up to capital ships like a British battleship. All seven heavy cruisers became casulaties during the course of the war.

ABOVE: Battleship, Littorio Class. Length was 776 feet with a displacement of 45,000 tons and a speed of 31 knots. The Regia Marina had ordered four of these relatively large battleships, but only 3 were completed before the armistice. Of the three built before the end of the war, one was sunk after the end of hostilities. They were considered to have good speed for their class, but had a low rate of fire and the secondary AA guns were not thought to be very good defense against attack from planes.

ABOVE: Battleship, Duilio Class. Length was 612 feet with a displacement of 29,000 tons and a speed of 28 knots. These capital ships were actually either built before or during the First World War, and then overhauled in the thrities and improved upon in many ways. As such their operational lifespan was lengthened and they proved to be effective ships during World War II, although by no means comparable to the younger, more modern battleships of the day.

BELOW: Italian & German supply convoys were constantly threatened by British air and naval forces, especially from units based in Malta.

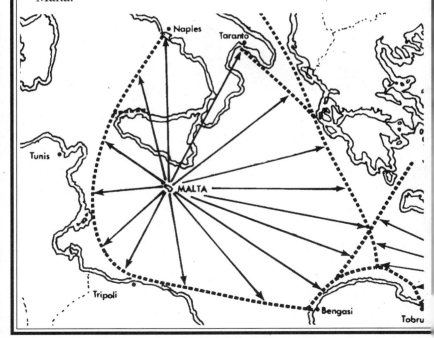

AXIS SUPPLY & REINFORCEMENTS TO LIBYA
June 1940 - December 1942
[A Compendium of Successful and Unsuccessful Transport of Men and Material to North Africa]

DATES	Troops Landed Safely*	Troops Sunk & Drowned*
June - September 1940	13,619	0
October 1940 - January 1941	27,925	252
February - June 1941	82,491	4,207
July - December 1941	48,303	7,921
January - June 1942	9,009	1,370
July - December 1942	7,851	1,186
Total (Libya only)	189,198	14,936
* These figures are for Italian merchant ships (not the small German merchant fleet that operated in the Mediterranean).		** In thousands of tons.

DATES	Equipment Landed**	Equipment Sunk**
June - September 1940	148,817	0
October 1940 - January 1941	197,742	7,712
February - June 1941	447,815	29,556
July - December 1941	356,294	95,487
January - June 1942	441,878	27,396
July - December 1942	337,409	119,780
Total (Libya only)	1,929,955	279,931

The above figures tells us in explicit detail just how important Allied interdiction of German and Italian supplies and reinforcements were during the North African campaign. The numbers of men lost equalled one full strength German division (15,000 men), while the tonnage lost was considerable (almost 13% of all equipment and supplies shipped to Africa). This equipment included such items as tanks, trucks, spare parts, munitions, planes, clothing, food, water and just about everything needed to sustain life (and to take life) in the desert. Had these thousands of tons of supplies, men, and other war material which were sunk, reached Libya unharmed, the effect on the course of the campaign would have been significant. Again our eyes are drawn to Malta.

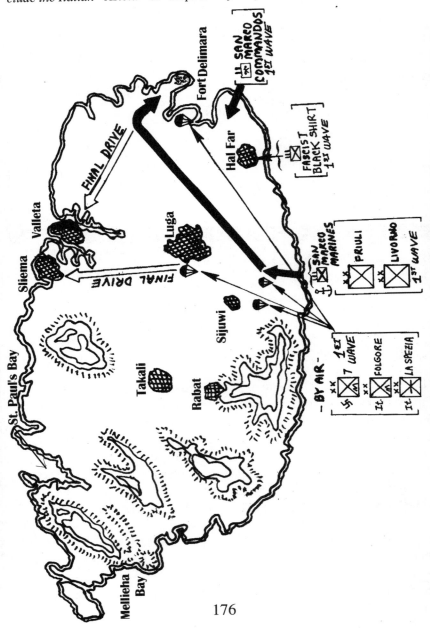

BELOW: The planned invasion of Malta, as conceived by a joint German and Italian command. The first wave units are pictured, as well as the assault sites. Secondary drives are shown as "final drive" lines. Follow up units would include the Italian "Asieta" & "Napoli" Infantry Divisions.

occasions Malta almost fell but managed to hold on. Whenever the Axis planned a major attack or were in difficulties in North Africa the Italo-German airforces endeavoured to put Malta out of action..

An air and sea assault was planned on Malta in 1942, codenamed C3. Training began in April involving a combined Italo-German airborne and seaborne attack force comprising the German 7th Paratroops, the Italian Folgore Paratroop Division and La Spezia Air-Transportable Division for the airborne phase of the operation. For the seaborne phase, the Friuli, Livorno, Assietta, Napoli and Superga Infantry Divisions (the later earmarked for the invasion of Gozo, a 67 sq km island to the north-west of the main island), elements of the 10th Armored Regiment, San Marco Marines, Italian airforce assault and ground troops plus Blackshirt battalions - a force that totalled 96,000 men and approximately 1500 aircraft.

The operation was cancelled in June 1942 when Rommel (with Hitler's approval) opposed the operation as it was felt it would dangerously reduce the flow of much needed supplies for his advance into the Nile and the expected occupation of Cairo. The Naples-Tripoli route was the most important passage for the convoys supplying Libya. Those departing Naples had a choice of two routes - one through the Strait of Messina which, like others from Taranto and Brindisi, proceeded towards Tripoli or Bengasi. They had to steam dangerously close to Malta which represented, with its submarines and torpedo bombers, a lethal threat.

Efforts were made by the Italian and German air forces to neutralise the 246 sq km island, but results were erratic and the threat was never fully removed. To minimise the risk from Malta, an alternative route from Naples went around Sicily, stopping there at Trapani or Palermo, then coasting Tunisia near the Kerkennah sand banks and the isle of Djerba. Another used was Taranto-Brindisi-Navarino (Greece)-Bengasi-Tobruch. This carried the convoys away from Malta, but within range of British airfields in Egypt.

As the majority of convoys arrived in Tripoli, transportation to the front line by road was a long and arduous undertaking. Use was made of coastal shipping when possible to carry troops and equipment between Bengasi, Tobruch, Bomba and Derna, and El Alamein in Egypt. The Athens-Crete-Tobruch route was mainly used by German transports to supply Crete and North Africa with men and equipment.

Supplies were vital for the continuation of operations in Africa. British military intelligence basing their estimate on the Brescia Division surmised that it took 172 tonnes of supplies a day to keep an Italian infantry division in the field, of this figure 15 1/4 tonnes was for food (1 1/2 kg per man) and 64 tonnes for ammunition and ordinance.

In the three years supplies were shipped to Libya, the navy escorted 1210 convoys. It lost 4 cruisers, 14 destroyers, 12 destroyer escorts, 10 submarines and 47 auxiliary vessels. The merchant navy lost 342 ships. Although during this period the number of vessels sunk was high, only 14% of all cargo was lost and 90% of the troops transported by sea landed safely. The discrepancy between the high loss of shipping and the relatively small percentage of cargo lost was because many vessels were sunk while in port.

Approximately 40% of the axis shipping tonnage sunk is credited by some sources to be due to have been achieved by the use of ULTRA by the British to intercept signals about convoy sailing's. The Italians did not rely on cypher machines to the extent the Germans did, instead employing book cyphers for which British code breakers could not crack. The Italians did however, from early 1941 employ a machine known to the British as C-38, but it was not as sophisticated as the Enigma machines, its codes were soon broken. The intercepted information from the C-38 provided invaluable data on North African shipping movements.

INSET: *Arrival of the Germans. Germans occupy an Italian fort on the Gulf of Sidra (at Msus)- March/April 1941.*
- David Hunter

GERMAN REINFORCEMENTS

From the day Italy entered the war Germany had been offering aid to fight the British in Africa. This included the supply of 250 Pz III and IV tanks and help in building a plant to produce PZ IIIs and IVs. The proposal was turned down by Mussolini because he wanted his victory to be a purely Italian one. He was also under pressure from Italian industrialist to keep all war profits at home.

Before the abortive Italian invasion of Egypt plans, had already been prepared by Germany as early as August 1940 to send a panzer corps, drawn from the 3rd and 5th Panzer Divisions and the 13 Motorized Infantry Division, to North Africa. In October 1940 Hitler promised Mussolini a panzer brigade and the VIII Fliegerkorps for a reopening of the Egyptian offensive, on the 12 or 13th of that month, but Marshal Graziani could not be moved and the reinforcements were not sent.

Chief of the German General Staff, General Franz Halder, then sent Major-General Wilhelm von Thoma to Libya to undertake a personal inspection of conditions there. He reported to Hitler in October 1940 that because of the difficulty of supplying an army in Libya, four panzer divisions was the maximum that could be supported. He thought it was also the minimum force to ensure success. Hitler, however, was adamant only one panzer division could be spared. In November he ordered one be held in readiness for use in North Africa if necessary.

Hitler and his army staff officers had a continental outlook to their strategy and did not attach adequate importance to the Mediterranean at the time, considering it merely a secondary theatre. The main British sea route that brought vital food, raw materials and military reinforcements from the British dominions passed through the Red sea, Suez Canal and the Mediterranean. Known as "the lifeline of the British Empire", to cut this route would mean shipping would have to go around Africa via the Cape of Good Hope, which took twice as long. The ideal

LEFT: General Erwin Rommel, newly appointed commander of the German Afrika Korps.   - Author's Collection.

A column of German army vehicles belonging to forward elements of the newly arrived armored blocking force line the sides of a Tripoli street, February, 1941.

- Achille Rastelli

place to sever this vital artery was in the Mediterranean.

When the December 1940 offensive led to a series of severe reversals, the Italian High Command requested German troops be sent to their assistance, overturning their previous request for raw materials and equipment only. The Luftwaffe X Fliegerkorps was ordered to Italy from Norway, and arrived in Sicily in late December 1940 to operate against Allied shipping and to patrol the sea lanes between Italy and Libya. In the wake of the Italian defeats Hitler held a special conference with the chiefs of his armed forces on January 9, 1941 at the Berghof, after which he said:

"The loss of the Libyan area must be prevented under all circumstances. The loss of this colony would not entail very far-reaching military consequences, because it would neither substantially increase the danger of air attacks on Italy nor affect the situation in French North Africa. However, the British forces committed in Egypt would then be freed for other tasks and, above all, the effect on Italian morale would be extremely unfavourable.

"Obviously, the Italians are not able to resist the British without our support. This is due not so much to their inferiority as soldiers as their lack of modern defensive weapons against the British tanks. These tanks, no doubt will be worn out soon as a result of constant driving through the sands. The Tripolitanian area offers better chances to block the roads, but the Italians lack the equipment needed for this purpose. It is, therefore, necessary to support them at least to an extent which will enable them to hold out for the next few months. Then the hot season will set in, during which the British tanks will no longer be able to operate."

After this pronouncement it was decided to send immediately a German army formation to Libya (codename Operation Sunflower) comprising a armoured blocking force, the 5th Light Division (a composite division made up of one panzer regiment [drawn from 3rd Pz.Div] and ancillary mechanised units) to hold

ABOVE: Comradeship between Axis soldiers, as a sergeant in the Italian Carabinieri lights the cigarette of his German ally.

- Author's Collection.

The arrival of the Afrika Korps in early 1941allowed the Italian forces in Libya to regroup and, aided by the Germans, once again retake the initiative in North Africa.

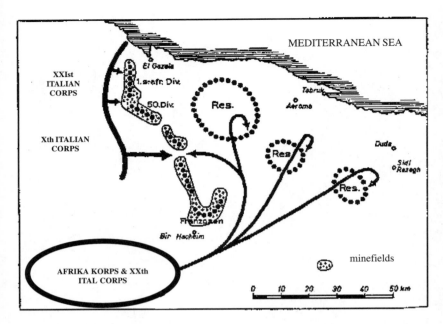

MEDITERRANEAN SEA

XXIst ITALIAN CORPS

Xth ITALIAN CORPS

El Gazala

1. arafr. Div.

50. Div.

Res.

Tobruk

Acroma

Res.

Duda

Sidi Rezegh

Res.

Franzosen

Bir Hacheim

minefields

AFRIKA KORPS & XXth ITAL CORPS

0 10 20 30 40 50 km

ABOVE: The fall of Tobruk in the fall of 1940 was avenged later when, with the help of the "Deutsches Afrika Korps", the Italian army was able to reconquer this important port city, along with eastern Libya.

RIGHT: Signal engineers run out a telephone line in Egypt, August 28th, 1942.
- Author's Collection

184

ABOVE: Combat laden Italian infantry march under the watch-ful eyes of General Erwin Rommel.

- Rudy D'Angelo.

BELOW: General Rommel and General Azzi of the 101st Trieste Motorized Infantry Division follow the course of the battle for the conquest of Tobruk, June 23rd 1942.

- Bundesarchiv Koblenz.

THE END IN TRIPOLI, 1943

ABOVE: General Montgomery dictating terms to the Lt. Governor and other officials of Tripoli town and Tripolitania at Castel Benito. Tripoli was occupied by the Allies on January 23rd, 1943. For all intents and purposes, the war in Libya was over.

- ATL, Wellington, NZ

the British advance. Forward elements began to arrive in Tripoli on February 14 1941. Plans were also made to transfer the 15th Panzer Division, the bulk of which arrived in April. 1941. The newly-appointed commander of the German ground forces in Libya was 50-year-old General Erwin Rommel, a resourceful, determined and successful panzer commander appointed personally by Hitler. Rommel arrived in Libya on February 12, barely six days after being informed of his new command.

He was nominally under the command of General Italo Gariboldi. During the period that the Germans and Italians fought together in Africa, many friendships developed between men of the two armies, though this happened more between officers than among the lower ranks because of language difficulties. Contact at the personal level was not always easy and combat units were not mixed due to problems in communications as well as logistical and other organizational incompatibilities. However, in order to stiffen some Italian units at Tobruch in 1941, and at El Alamein in 1942, Rommel used German troops in company or even battalion strength to reinforce them, but these were the only occasions when German and Italian soldiers fought in close proximity for any length of time.

The German troops did make an effort communicate with their Italian allies is shown by the large number of Italian language classes attended by German soldiers, and by the number of Italian-German grammar and phrase books found among the possessions of German POWs. With the arrival of the Germans, an odyssey began in which the Italians no longer fought as an independent army, but were reliant on their German ally to bolster the defense of the Italian colony. Now events often beyond the Italians control guided the North African war, one in which was to see the Italo-German army reach the gates of Alexandria in Egypt at the height of its glory, and to then ignominiously have to withdraw from Libya after almost two years of toilsome see-saw battles, mostly confined to the narrow coastal strips of Libya and Egypt.

ABOVE: Bersaglieri dug into position in the region of El Alamein, 1 November, 1942.

- Author's Collection.

BELOW: Paratroopers of the 185th Folgore Paratroop Division being searched after their capture; Most likely at Deir Abu al Hadiya, November 6th, 1942.

- Taranaki Museum, NZ

ABOVE: Australians bury Italian dead at El Alamein.
                                              - Dal McGuirk.

BELOW: The German cemetery at Mersa Matruh held more than one thousand crosses. These mark the graves of men who paid the price of the Axis war in that small part of North Africa.
                          - SA National Museum of Military History

Epilogue

On January 23rd, 1943 the British rolled into Tripoli, and *Libia Italiana* ceased to exist. The Italians, after leaving blood, sweat and tears in what was once called "the bucket of sand" had evacuated the city. Defeat turned to resignation. Tripolitania and Cirenaica were now under the military administration of Great Britain and the Fezzan region came under France. The peace treaty signed by Italy in February 1947 stipulated that Italy had to renounce all claims to her former colony, but the situation was far from settled.

There existed no independent factions in Libya to guarantee a new government and thus the United Nations controlled the administration of Libya until 1951. At that time, a federated and independent Libya was constituted, formed from the three provinces of Fezzan, Cirenaica and Tripolitania. The new nation proclaimed its independence on 24 December 1951. Sayid Mohommed Idris al-Mahdi Al Senussi rose to the throne. The newly crowned King Idris, as he was now known, had been living in Egypt since he escaped the Italian repression of the Senussi and remained there until 1947 when the British brought him back as the Emir of Cirenaica.

King Idris proved to be inept and despotic, and feudal conflicts resurfaced in Libya. In the early to mid-1950's, the United States and Great Britain, in exchange for military bases in Liyba, agreed to provide the Libyan government with food, other goods, and financial support. These amenities however, never reached the Libyan poor. Instead it went to the pockets of King Idris and his vast group of friends and family. In 1955, France withdrew her forces from the Fezzan. The same year, Libya became a member of the United Nations. In 1956 a new treaty between Italy and Libya was signed, to pay Libya for war damages and to recognize the properties occupied by Italians who emigrated to Libya. Also in 1955, Standard Oil (later Exxon) began drilling for oil. In 1959, the American giant discovered the vast reserves at Bir

Zelten in Cirenaica, and the Gulf of Sirte. By 1960, other Anglo-Americans joined the explorations and the world production and commercialization of Libyan petroleum was underway. Due to the archaic structure of the monarchy, it was not capable of doing what was best for its people with its new found wealth. Rocco Amedeo DiProspero an Italian colonist living in Libya recounts his experience of this time:

"By January 1943, there was no more 'Libia Italiana' per say and we all cried tears of bitterness. It was a sad time, it was like we were losing all we had worked for, but my father did not want to go back to Italy, this was his home now and he was willing to see what happened after the war. Italy signed treaties back and forth, but life pretty much ran the same on the farm and our ranch.

"By 1951 the writing was on the wall. The three provinces of Tripolitania, Cirenaica and Fezzan formed 'Libia Indipendente' and King Idris took over.

"What a disaster he was, an idiot. Figlio di puttane, after all we did for his country, he started to take it back into the middle ages.

"Hostility began towards us and in some areas we heard that some Italians who resisted the Libyans were killed. Instead of going forward, as Libya did under Balbo, it was going backwards. Controls were up everywhere, it was more uncertain than during the war itself.

"Then in 1955, they took our land, we got nothing, no enumeration, it was as if we owned not a blessed thing and that we had somehow done all this for nothing. No money, no real estate, no passage home, nothing. We left Tripoli in March 1955, with the shirts on our backs! A few suitcases. Nothing else! My father had been given two choices either leave Libya with nothing, or you can stay in Libya, renounce Italian citizenship and work for the state, which will take over our farm and all you own. He said "Va a fan' gulo! and we decided to leave. That was that."

In September 1969, a group of Socialist minded officers launched a coup d'etat which overthrew King Idris and declared a "Revolutionary Republic." The intentions of the young officers were noble: to raise the Libyan people to a new social status and share in the wealth of the country's resources.

In January 1970, an Army captain and a Bedouin, Muhammar el-Ghaddafi, was elected President. The new Libyan leader denounced the treaties with England and the United States, ordering the closure of western military bases, nationalizing all foreign owned lands, declaring them to be Libyan property. He also annulled the 1956 treaty with Italy, confiscated Italian property in the former colony, and expelled all Italians from Libya. He even went so far as to order the removal of bodies of thousands of Italian soldiers buried in the country. Many foreign banks were expelled and the remainder nationalized as were the oil companies. Libya also began to collaborate with the Soviet Union, turning her back on her former allies.

- Rudy D'Angelo

Milizia della Libia

LEFT: The Italian Fascist symbol.

BELOW: A memorial erected to commemorate the 4th Libyan Black-shirt Division "3 Gennaio." The engine and rear fuselage of a shot down Italian aircraft has been added to the stone.
- Author's collection

LEFT: Italian Cross of Military Merit.

All these illustrations, courtesy of the Keith Williams Collection.

LEFT: Italian Order of the Crown Knight.

RIGHT: Italian Campaign Medal.

194

BIBLIOGRAPHY

World Aircraft, Commercial Aircraft 1935-1960 By Enzo Angelucci and Paolo Matricardi. Sampson Low, United Kingdom. 1979.

Uniforms and Traditions of the German Army 1933-1945 By John R. Angola and Adolf Schlicht Vol 3. R. James Bender Publishing. California USA. 1992.

Mezzi Dell' Esercito Italiano 1935-1945 By Ugo Barlozzetti and Alberto Pirella. Editoriale Olimpia. Firenze Italy. 1986.

The Desert Generals by Corelli Barnett. William Kimber. London. 1960.

Rommel's Intelligence in the Desert campaign by Hans-Otto Behrendt. William Kimber & Co. London. 1985.

Uniform, Organisation and History of the Afrika Korps by Roger James Bender and Richard D. Law. R. James Bender Publishing, San Jose, California USA. 1986.

Armi Portatili Artiglierie e Somoventi Del Regio Esercito Italiano 1900-1943 By Giulio Benussi. Intergest Milano, Italy. 1975.

Armor Camouflage & Markings North Africa 1940-43, Volume One by George R. Bradford. Preston, Ontario, Canada. 1971.

Alamein 1933 - 1962 An Italian Story By Paolo Caccia - Dominioni. George Allen & Unwin Ltd. London, United Kingdom. 1966.

Historical Dictionary of Fascist Italy by Philip V. Cannistraro. Greenwood Press, Westport Connecticut. 1982.

Streets, Critical Perspectives on Public Space Edited by Zeynep Celik, Diane Favro and Richard Ingersoll. University of California Press, Berkeley and Los Angeles .1994

Afrika Korps 1941-42 by Peter Chamberlian and Chris Ellis. Almark Publishing Co. Ltd. London. 1976.

Il Reggimento "Giovani Fascisti" Nella Campagna Dell' Africa Settentrionale 1941-1943 By Antonio Cioci. Edizioni Ari, Italy.

Grafiche Elleci, Bologna Italy. 1980.

Submarines Attacking by Admiral Aldo Cocchia. William Kimber London, United Kingdom. 1956.

The War in the Desert By Richard Collier. Time-Life Books Inc. USA. 1977.

Historical Le Uniformi Coloniali Libiche 1912-1942 by Piero Crociani and Andrea Viotti. La Roccia Edizioni, Roma Italy. 1980.

The Brutal Friendship: Mussolini, Hitler, and the fall of Italian Fascism by F. W. Deakin. Penguin Books Ltd. England. 1966.

A Nest of Corsairs: The Fighting Karamanli's of Tripoli 1711-1835 by Seton Dearden. John Murray Ltd. London. 1970.

Encylopedia of Tanks by Duncan Crow and Robert J. Icks. Chartwell Books Inc. USA. 1975

Encylopedia of Armoured Cars and Halftracks by Duncan Crow and Robert J. Icks. Chartwell Books Inc. USA. 1976.

World War Two Tanks by George Forty. Osprey, Great Britain. 1995.

PAI Polizia Dell'Africa Italiana by Raffaele Girlando, Italia Editrice. Campobasso, Italy. 1996

Italiani...tutti in divisia! By Elio and Vittorio del Giudice. Tuttostoria, Parma, Italy. 1980.

Mare Nostrum The War in the Mediterranean by Jack Greene. Watsonville California, USA. 1990.

German, Italian & Japanese Fighters of World War II by Bill Gunston. Salamander Books Ltd, United Kingdom. 1980.

Bombers of World War II by Bill Gunston. Salamander Books Ltd, United Kingdom. 1980.

The First Three Years of the War by Harold Hobson. Hutchinson, United Kingdom. The Long *Range Desert Group* by W. B. Kennedy Shaw.Greenhill Books, London. 1989.

Italian State Railways Steam Locomotives by P. M. Kalla-Bishop. Tourret Publishing. England. 1986.

Long Range Desert Group by W. B. Kennedy Shaw. Greenhill Books, London 1989.

The Rommel Papers Edited by B. H. Liddell Hart. Collins, London, United Kingdom. 1953.

Italy in Africa by Christopher Hollis. Hamish Hamilton, London, United Kingdom. 1953.

Desert My Dwelling Place By Lt. Col. David Lloyd Owen.Cassell and Company ltd. England. 1957.

Providence Their Guide The Long Range Desert Group 1940-45 by David Lloyd Owen. Harrap London. 1980.

Australia In The War 1939-45. Army. To Benghazi by Gavin Long. Canberra Australia War Memorial. 1952.

I Paracadutisti Italiani 1937/45 by Giuseppe Lundari and Pietro Compagni. Editrice Militare Italiana. Milano, Italy. 1989.

Rommel Battles And Campaigns by Kenneth Macksey. Arms and Armour Press, London, United Kingdom. 1979.

The Battle for the Mediterranean by Donald Macintyre. B.T. Batsford London 1964.

Beda Fomm the classic victory by Kenneth Macksey. Ballantine Books, United Kingdom 1979.

Roman North Africa. by E. Lennox Manton. B. A. Seaby Ltd, London, United Kingdom. 1988. Official History of New Zealand in the Second World War 1939-45.

Prisoners of War by W. Wynne Mason. War History Branch Department of Internal Affairs Wellington, New Zealand. 1954.

Australia In The War 1939-45. Series I Vol III. Tobruk and El Alamein by Barton Maughan. Canberra. 1966.

North African Handbook 1994. Edited by Anne and Keith McLachlan. Trade and Travel Publications. England. 1993.

Afrikakorps Self Portrait by Dal McGuirk. Airlife, United Kingdom. 1992.

Rommel's Army in Africa by Dal McGuirk. Stanley Paul, London, United Kingdom. 1987.

African Trilogy by Alan Moorehead. Hamish Hamilton, London, United Kingdom. 1946.

Ciano's Diary 1939-1943. William Heinemann Ltd, London. 1947.

Roma 1943 by Paolo Monelli. Longanesi. Milano, Italy. 1963.

Gadaffi The Desert Mystic. By George Tremlett. Carroll & Graf. USA. 1993.

Le Operazioni In Africa Settentrionale. Vol 1 Sidi El Barrani (Giugno 1940-Febbraio 1941). By Mario Montanari. Stato Maggiore Dell Esercito Ufficio Storico. Rome 1990.

Le Operazioni In Africa Settentrionale. Vol II Tobruk (Marzo 1941-Gennaio 1942). By Mario Montanari. Stato Maggiore Dell Esercito Ufficio Storico. Rome 1993.

Le Operazioni In Africa Settentrionale. Vol III El Alamein (Gennaio-Novembre 1942). By Mario Montanari. Stato Maggiore Dell Esercito Ufficio Storico. Rome 1989.

Le Operazioni In Africa Settentrionale. Vol IV Enfidaville (Novembre 1942-Maggio 1943). By Mario Montanari. Stato Maggiore Dell Esercito Ufficio Storico. Rome 1993.

Land Battles: North Africa, Sicily, and Italy by Trevor Nevitt Dupuy. Edmund Ward Publishers, London, United Kingdom. 1964.

Taranto By Don Newton & A. Cecil Hampshire. New English Library. England. 1974.

L'Italia e Piccola? Terre D'Oltremare Volume Secondo by Francesco Ogliari. Cavallotti Editori, Milano Italy. 1981.

L'Italia e Piccola? Terre D'Oltremare Volume Terzo By Francesco Ogliari. Cavallotti Editori, Milano Italy. 1981.

L'Italia e Piccola? Terre D'Oltremare Volume Quarto by Francesco Ogliari. Cavalloti Editori, Milano Italy. 1981.

L'Italia e Piccola? Terre D'Oltremare Volume Sesto By Francesco Ogliari. Cavallotti Editori, Milano Italy. 1981

Le Divise del Duce by Ugo Pericoli. Rizzoli, Milano. 1983

German Fighters over the Med by Bryan Philpott. Patrick Stephens Ltd. United Kingdom. 1981

Artigliere e Auto Mezzi Dell' Esercito Italiano Nella Seconda Guerra Mondiale by Nicola Pignato. Ermanno Albertelli Editore, Parma Italy. 1972.

Dallo Alla Divisia La Marina Mercantile Italiana dal 1932 al

1945. Transporti Marittimi Di Linea Volume Quinto By Lamberto Radogna, Francesco Ogliari, Achille Rastelli and Alessandro Zenoni. Milano 1984.

Italian Tanks And Fighting Vehicles Of World War 2 by Ralph Riccio. Pique Publications, United Kingdom. 1977.

MVSN, 1923-1943, Badges and Uniforms of the Italian Fascist Militia by Guido Rosignoli. Farnham Surrey England. 1980.

With Rommel In The Desert by Heinz W. Schmidt. Harrap London, United Kingdom. 1980.

Battle for Egypt. The summer of 1942. By J. L. Scouller. War History Branch, Department of Internal Affairs, Wellington New Zealand. 1955.

Italo Balbo A Fascist Life By Claudio G. Segre. University of California Press, Berkley Los Angles, London. 1987.

Fourth Shore by Claudio G. Segre. The University of Chicago Press, Chicago and London. 1974.

Regia Aeronautica Vol 1. by Christopher Shores. Squadron/Signal Publication. Texas, USA. 1976.

Mussolini's Soldiers by Rex Trye. Airlife Publishers, Shropshire, England. 1995.

Biographical Dictionary of World War II by Christopher Tunney. J.M. Dent & Sons Ltd. London. 1972.

Italian Foreign Policy under Mussolini by Luigi Villari. The Devin-Adair Company. USA. 1956

World War 2 combat uniforms and insignia by Martin Windrow. Patrick Stephens. Cambridge, United Kingdom. 1977.

Rommels Desert Army by Martin Windrow. Osprey Publishing Ltd. London United Kingdom. 1976.

Rommel By Desmond Young. Collins London, United Kingdom. 1950.

PERIODICALS

AFV-G2 Magazine. Volume 6, Number 9. January-February 1980. The Italian M11/39 Medium Tank by James Steuard.

Command Military History, Strategy & Analysis. Issue 20. Jan-Feb 1993. The Summer of '42 The proposed Axis invasion of Malta by Jack Greene & Alesandro Massignani.

Europa. No 41, Vol VIII, No1. 1995. Raggrupamento Esplorante in North Africa by Paul E. Bove.

ITreni. No36, February 1984. Treni italiani in libia fotografati durante la guerra. *Oggi Magazine*. Supplement No.45, 6 November 1952.

Storia e Dossier. Anno III Luglio/agosto 1988 n.20

Fil-Italia. Volume XXIV, no1. Winter 1997/98.

DOCUMENTS

Public Record Office.
WO, War Office Collection.
WO33/2726, Order of Battle Italian Forces in Libya, April 1940.
WO33/2727, Order of Battle Italian Forces in Libya, August 26 1940.
WO33/2729, Order of Battle Italian Forces in Libya, July 1941.
WO106/2044, Italian 22nd Army Corps Instructions for the defence of Libya, 31 March 1940.
WO106/2072, War Diary of 2nd Lt Federico Corio.
WO106/2118, Occupation of Sollum and Halfaya pass by Italians, September 1940.
WO106/2129, Captured Italian documents received from M.I.3b 26/8/41.
WO208/39, Maintenance reports of an Italian Division in Libya.
WO208/40, Battle strengths of enemy forces in Africa.
WO208/4528, Order of Battle Italian Forces in Libya, January 1942.
WO230/248, Land Tenure In Cyrenaica 1948.

Documents pertaining to the Italian armed forces in North Africa from the New Zealand National Archives. War History Collection.

MS#C-065f. English copy. Africa, 1941 By Helmuth Greiner. Historical Division European Command. Foreign Military Studies Branch. 1946.

Unpublished research documents from the Richard Garczynski and Christopher Coleman archives.

Transcript of lecture as supplied on Internet World Wide Web Page by Mark Lomas on a talk given by Sir Harry Hinsley, Tuesday 19th October 1993 at Babbage Lecture Theatre, Computer Laboratory, UK. On the influence of ULTRA in the Second World War.

Pre-War And Wartime Publications

Cirenaica Illustrata July-August 1932, January 1933, February 1933, July-August 1934, September 1934.

Libia Rivista Mensile Illustrata. Anno IV - N 5-6-7-8. May-August 1940. Tripoli.

From Tripoli to Gadames. Ente Turistico Alberghiero Della Liba

Militargeographische Beschreibung von Nordost - Afrika text und Bildheft. Generalstab der Heeres. Berlin 1940.

Marsch und Kampf des Deutschen Afrikakorps. Band 1. 1941. Carl Rohrig Verlag, Kom.-Ges/Munchen.

Heros du Desert La Lutte en Afrique du Nord Par Hanns Gert Freiherr von Esebeck. 1942.

Helden der Wuste. Verlag die Heimbucherei. Berlin. 1943.

Mit Rommel in der Wuste by Wilhelm Wessel. Bildgut Verlag, Essen. 1943

General feldmarschall Rommel und der Feldzug in Nordafrika. Erasmusdruk Berlin. 1943.

Ministero Delle Colonie. Regolamento Per Le Uniformi Coloniali Del Ministro E Del Sottosegretario Di Stato Per Le Colonie E Per e Uniformi Dei Funzionari Coloniali Del Ruolo

Di Governo. Rome 1937.

Stati e Colonie Libia 1937- XV, Di Politica Internazional, Milano

Janes Fighting Ships 1939. Sampson Low, Marston and & Co. Ltd. London. 1939.

Middle East Training Pamphlet No.10. Lessons of Cyrenaica Campaign. December 1940 - February 1941.

The Road To The Nile by Wilson Macarthur. Collins London and Glasgow. 1941.

Handbook On The Italian Army. May 1943. Army Map Service. U.S. Army. Reprinted by Athena Books. United Kingdom. 1983.

The conquest of North Africa. Burke Publishing Co. Ltd. London. 1944.

ABOUT THE AUTHOR

Rex Trye is the author of the respected ground breaking book, "Mussolini's Soldiers." He has been a researcher and collector of Italian miltiary items for the past 25 years. He is honorary curator of the Italian collection at the Queen Elizabeth 2nd Army Memorial Musem in Waiouru, New Zealand.

He is also a contributing writer to the Axis Europa magazine, as well as other historical publications.

He works for the computer department of the local newspaper company in his home town of New Plymouth, New Zealand.

He is married to Katherine and has two children, Maggie and Leif.

Color Plate Descriptions

PARATROPOPER, 1942. This paratrooper is a member of the 186th Parachute Infantry Regiment of the 185th "Folgore" Parachute Division. He is wearing the model 1942 khaki tunic and trousers with the distinct wing and dagger insignia of the parachute arm on his tunic lapels, and the jump qualification badge on his left upper arm.

On his head head has a model 1941 jump helmet with camouflage cover. On his feet he is wearing the black leather jump boots with rubber soles. His side arm consists of a model 1939 fighting knife and a model 38A 9mm Beretta submachine gun, which was a popular weapon with Italian airborne soldiers.

LIBYAN DESERT SOLDIER, 1940. This Sahariana wears a crimson colored cummerbund around his waist which denotes that he belongs to the 5th Sahariana Group. His rank is that of *Bulucbasci* (sergeant), a name that is a vestige of the former Turkish rulers. The natural leather ammunition pouches worn are a style which was popular with desert troops. The khaki turban was often wrapped around the face to protect against the extremes in desert temperatures. His trousers are the comfortable loose fitting white cotton trousers known as sirual, leather sandals are worn on the feet.

BACK OF DUST JACKET:

BLACKSHIRT MILITIAMAN, 1940. This member of the "28 Ottobre" Blackshirt Division wears on his collars the double black flame with brass Fascio's which indicate he is a member of the militia. On his left arm is displayed a stamped aluminum divisional shield of the division. On the belt is the model 1935 dagger and leather tool pouch for his model 1930 6.5mm Breda light machinegun. He wears black puttees with white rolled down socks which was a distinct feature of a militia man as was the black felt fez worn on the head.

FRONT OF DUST JACKET:

ARTILLERYMAN, 1941. This soldier belongs to the 12th Artillery Regiment of the 55th "Savona" Infantry Division. He is wearing the grey-green woolen tunic with black collar, the single orange flame with a five pointed star, shows he belongs to a branch of the royal army artillery. He wears the model 1935 pith helmet with brass artillery badge and rosette of the Italian colors. His equipment consists of a model 1891 two pocket bandoleer and a model 1891 Carcano 6.5mm rifle.

Arab Fascist Youth cap badge, with the initials of the movement, which was "Gioventu Araba del Littorio". The Fascist symbol lay atop the cap badge, along with two crossed rifles. Underneath was the crescent moon of Islam, as all the members were Moslem.

Arab Fascist Youth cloth badge. this was the identification badge of the Arab Fascist Youth, which was worn above the breast pocket of the tunic.

Front cover of a 1942 issue of "Tempo" (Time) Magazine, with a fine photographic study of a Bersaglieri soldier in typical desert uniform.

About *Axis Europa*

Axis Europa was established in January, 1995 by military historian and author, Antonio J. Munoz. The company was formed because of what seemed to be ageneral lack of readily available data on the "minor" Axis forces which fought on the side of Germany during the Second World War. The term "minor" Axis is deceptive, since our research has brought to light facts which make it perfectly clear that without these so-called "minor" forces, Germany could not have sustained her war effort for as long as she did.

The company publishes books dealing strictly with the subject of World War II Axis Military History. We do not cover the political or social aspects since there are sufficient books and magazines that cover these two aspects. We are **not** revisionists! We are only concerned with covering the military history of the Axis forces from an objective and un-biased point of view. We also publish a color journal dealing with the same subject matter. Our author's come from various countries: the US, Canada, Britain, The Netherlands, Finland, Italy, Croatia, etc.

The company has recently published its first ever purely German-oriented book ("The German Police"). In the future, we plan on producing more such books. Axis Europa fills a gap which no other firm has attempted to cover before: The field of NEW data on the military history of the Axis forces. One of our specialties is the sub-topic of foreign volunteers of the Wehrmacht and Waffen-SS. This is a fascinating area of study dealing with a huge foreign volunteer movement. We offer many titles on this particular subject.

We hope that once you see our list of books and magazines, you will agree with us that our line is unique and an important contribution to the military history of the Second World War.

Antonio J. Munoz
Publisher.

AXIS EUROPA

53-20 207th Street, Bayside, New York 11364-1716 USA

"Your one source for new and unique books & magazines on the military history of the axis forces in World War II"

Our color journal, "Axis Europa," is completely dedicated to this topic and to current book reviews on the same subject!

(sample copies are only $8.00 domestic, $9.00 Canadian, or $10.00 Overseas customers)

NOTE: FOR OVERSEAS AIR MAIL - Each book weighs approximately ½ pound each, except book numbers "1," "11," and "16" which weigh 4 pounds each.

Domestic: Book Rate: $5.00 1st book, $2.00 each additional; USPS Priority: $6.00 1st book, $3.00 each additional book. UPS Ground: 8.00 1st book, $3.00 each additional book.

Canadian: Surface charges are $4.00 for the 1st book, $3.00 each additional book. Air Mail (use Overseas Air mail rates, below).

Overseas: Surface - $10.00 for the 1st book, $3.00 each additional. BOOK DEALERS & STORES: Please check M-Bag rates (Call for quotes).

AIR MAIL OVERSEAS: 1 lb.= $7.20/ 2 lbs.= $12.00/ 3 lbs.= $16.80/ 4 lbs.= $21.60 5 lbs.= $26.40/ 6 lbs.= $31.20/ 7 lbs.= $36.00/ 8 lbs.= $40.80 9 lbs.= $45.60/ 10 lbs.= $50.40/ 11 lbs.= $55.20/ 12 lbs.= $64.48

Example: If you ordered one copy of Book No.11 and one copy each of book Nos. 2, 5, 9, & 10, the total (approximate) weight of your package would be 6 lbs. (pounds). The cost to ship AIR MAIL overseas would therefore be

$31.20 .**NOTE: Air Mail shipping to Pacific Rim & Middle Eastern countries is 10% higher,** so this 6 lb. package would cost $34.32 to send to a country like New Zealand, or Saudi Arabia (as examples).

Terms of Sale: <u>All sales are final</u>. We accept a returned item only at our discretion and only after you have contacted us in writing. Please do not return any books or magazines without first writing to us and stating the problem. We will decide if the situation merits a refund and then we will only give CREDIT or PARTIAL CREDIT towards any other Axis Europa product. Re-stocking, re-packaging and end user
fees may apply.

NEW YORK STATE RESIDENTS: You MUST include local sales tax. Axis Europa must (like all NYS businesses) file form T-100 with the New York State Tax office every three months.

INSURANCE: Insurance is not available to foreign orders. We suggest that you order using AIR MAIL which is the safest form of shipping.Domestic insurance rates: If your order is under $100.00, then your insurance cost is $2.00. If your order is under $200.00, then your insurance cost is $3.00 . If you order under $300, then the insurance is $4.00

NOTE: WE ARE NOT RESPONSIBLE FOR UN-INSURED PARCELS.

AXIS EUROPA BOOKS
UNIQUE BOOKS ON THE MILITARY HISTORY OF THE AXIS FORCES, 1939-1945
53-20 207th Street, Bayside, NY 11364
fax orders: 1 (718) 229-1352
Phone Orders: (718) 423-9893
URL- **http://www.axiseuropa.com**
[NOTE: We are not a revisionist organization!]

BOOKS FOR SALE
1] FORGOTTEN LEGIONS: OBSCURE COMBAT FORMATIONS OF THE WAFFEN-SS, 1943-1945. by Antonio J. Munoz. 424 pages, hard cover, dust jacket, 104 photos, 64 maps. Details the many battle groups, divisions, & special units formed by the Waffen-SS. Many interesting first-person accounts, loaded with information on orders of battle, charts on manpower and casualties, foreign volunteers, etc. $58.00 ISBN- 0-87364-646-0

2] THE KAMINSKI BRIGADE: A HISTORY, 1941-1945. by Antonio J. Munoz. 64 pages, sc, color covers, 18 battle maps, 4 tables, and 31 extremely rare photos, 6 of which show the unit in Warsaw, Poland where it committed atrocities. Covers the complete & detailed history of the most effective & infamous collabora- tionist anti-partisan brigade formed by the Germans from Russian volunteers. Fully footnoted and documented! *"This book deserves to be on the shelf of the serious student of WWII"*- Ray Tapio, CRITICAL HIT. ISBN- 1-891227-02-5

3] LIONS OF THE DESERT: ARAB VOLUNTEERS IN THE GERMAN ARMY, 1941-1945. by Antonio J. Munoz. 36 pages, sc color covers, numerous maps & drawings, plus 21 extremely rare photos of these Arab volunteers. The complete history of these units in Russia, the Balkans, North Africa, Italy, and even in front of Berlin as the Third Reich was collapsing! Includes 7 super rare photos of the elusive Arab 845th Battalion!!! $18.00 ISBN- 1-891227-03-3

4] SLOVENIAN AXIS FORCES IN WORLD WAR II, 1941-1945 by Antonio **J.** Munoz. 12 Color and b&w Plate illustrations by renowned military artist, Vincent Wai! Full color covers, perfect binding (flat spine), 84 pages plus covers, 165 extremely rare photos (100 never before published!), 35 tables, maps, line drawings, etc. Covers the complete history of all Slovenian collaborationist forces allied to the Italians and Germans during the war. Includes the "Blue Guard," "White Guard," with the Village Guard & Legion of Death, Slovene National Army, Slovene Home Guard, Upper Carnolia Defense Force, ethnic-German Defense Militia Regiment Lower Styria, etc.! An excellent reference source not only on the military history, but the organization, weapons, uniform, and insignia of the Slovene Axis forces! $22.00 ISBN- 1-891227-04-1

5] FOR CROATIA & CHRIST: THE CROATIAN ARMY IN WORLD WAR II, 1941-1945. by Antonio J. Munoz. 80 pages, sc, color covers, numerous maps, tables, and photos. Complete history of the Croatian military, includir [OUT OF PRINT] itia, Croat-German Legion divisions, Italian excellent introduction by noted German milit r Neulen. Most complete English language study on the subject! $20.00 ISBN- 1-891227-05-X

6] HERAKLES & THE SWASTIKA: GREEK VOLUNTEERS IN THE GERMAN ARMY, POLICE & SS, 1943- 1945. by Antonio J. Munoz 68 pages, sc, color covers, 35 detailed maps, 36 very rare photos of these Greek collaborationist volunteers. Contains a wealth of data on Greek police, volunteer, and militia forces, troop locations, OB's, etc! A history which has never been detailed before, not even in the Greek language! $19.00
ISBN- 1-891227-06-8

7] FORGOTTEN LEGIONS BOOKLET by Antonio J. Munoz. This spiral bound booklet contains additional data that only surfaced after the publication of book 1] FORGOTTEN LEGIONS. Has 45+ pages with complete, referenced listings, and additional photographs. $17.00 NOTE: not recommended unless you own "FORGOTTEN LEGIONS" (book 1 above)
ISBN- 1-891227-07-6

8] THE HUNGARIAN ARMY & ITS MILITARY LEADERSHIP IN WWII by Andris Kursietis. 62 pages, sc, 50 photos, 3 maps, 7 Hungarian war posters (including recruiting posters for the 25th SS Hunyadi Division and even the Arrow Cross). Covers the complete history of the Hungarian officer corps and their impact on the army and its actions. Now in its 2nd, expanded edition! $18.00
ISBN- 1-891227-08-4

9] HITLER'S EASTERN LEGIONS, Volume I - THE BALTIC SCHUTZMANNSCHAFT. by Antonio J. Munoz. 96 pages, perfect binding with color covers, numerous detailed battle maps, 14 uniform plates by Sean Ryan. Covers the complete history of the Lithuanian, Latvian, and Estonian police, SS, Frontier Guard, *"Schuma"* & front battalions, regiments and army units which were raised by the Germans from 1941-1945. Much data on the anti-guerrilla war behind Army Group North. Also lists a complete, chronological listing of the history of these units. The 3-page index makes it easy to check all units. $21.00 Now in its 2nd printing with 36 additional pages of data!!!
ISBN- 1-891227-09-2

10] HITLER'S EASTERN LEGIONS, Volume II - THE OSTTRUPPEN by Antonio J. Munoz. Second volume in the series, this one on purely Russian and White Russian volunteer. 52 pages, sc color covers, 13 photos, full color shoulder board and collar insignia of these forces, 5 uniform plates by Sean Ryan, 4 maps, 3-page glos sary. Includes a complete, chronological listing of each battalion and regiment. $24.00

ISBN- 1-891227-10-6

11] THE GERMAN POLICE 442 pages, flat spine, sc color covers. Dozen's of rare maps, tables, photos, line drawings, etc.! Complete study on the history of the entire SS & Police system, including the military history of each battalion and regiment! *"Handsomely presented...must be consi- dered the Bible on the subject."*- Andris Kursietis, military historian. $42.00

ISBN- 1-891227-11-4

12] EASTERN TROOPS IN ZEELAND, THE NETHERLANDS, 1943-1945 by Hans Houterman. 102 pages, flat spine, glossy color covers, sc, numerous maps, photos, tables, appendices. Covers the history of these Russian units in the Netherlands. The maps list the location of all eastern battalions in the West! $28.00

ISBN- 1-891227-00-9

13] RUSSIAN VOLUNTEERS IN HITLER'S ARMY, 1941-1945 by Wladyslaw Anders. 60 pages, sc color covers, flat spine, col ills of the emblems, Detailed ROA officer postings, numerous rare photos. Entire history of Vlasov & the ROA (Russian Army of Liberation). $13.00

ISBN- 1-891227-01-7

14] HRVATSKI ORLOVI: PARATROOPERS OF THE INDE-PENDENT STATE OF CROATIA, 1942-45 by Josip Novak & David Spencer. 70 pages, hard cover with color dj, flat spine, @ 30 photos, appendices, color uniform plate, etc.! History of this formation in detail. $22.00

ISBN- 1-891227-13-0

15] CHETNIK: The Story of the Royal Yugoslav Army of the Homeland, 1941-1945. by Momcilo Dobrich. Complete history of the Chetnik forces in WWII. Includes numerous detailed Orders of Battle for various years and dates, maps, photos, etc. The appendices include a complete history (detailed as well) of the Serbian State & Frontier Guard, as well as the Montenegro Volunteer Corps! $17.95

ISBN- 1-891227-20-3

16] THE ROYAL HUNGARIAN ARMY 1920-1945 Volume I Organization & History. by Dr. Leo W. G. Niehorster Hard bound, with 100lb (heavy), glossy, full color dust jacket! This 317-page, hard

bound, and oversized book (8 ½" by 11") contains the military history of the Hungarian Army from 1920-1945: a period which has been described as *the most* exciting, dramatic, traumatic, and historically significant period in the entire history of the Magyar State. Containing a wealth of data such as orders of battle, schematic tables, & detailed battle maps to support the very exciting, lucid, and detailed text. Dr. Niehorster weaves the fabric history of the Hungarian Army like an expert. Having taken 20 years to complete, this first volume is all encompassing! The 2nd Volume will concentrate on the military equipment of the Hungarian Army as well as including a wealth of photographs. Volume II is slated for a 1999 release date. Buy this first, detailed military history for only $55.00 + s&h
ISBN-1-891227-19-X

WE ACCEPT ALL MAJOR CREDIT CARDS!

Place an order for any of these books and receive a FREE sample copy of our color journal. "Axis Europa", (Please be sure to mention special offer No.17).
Note: Shipping & handling costs are separate & will be billed to your account. Please specify if you wish air mail/ 1st Class or surface (ground/sea) shipping. We are NOT responsible for uninsured parcels.

WHOLESALE RATES
Who qualifies to be a wholesaler & book dealer? In an effort to help expand the distribution of our books and magazines, Axis Europa will not require that you show us proof of being in business (like a resale No.); But experience has taught us that if someone writes in saying that they are a book dealer, the chances are that indeeed they are. The "proof is in the pudding" when dealers order multiple copies of one book..
Our rates are based on a sliding scale. The larger the order, the bigger the discount. The great thing about our company is that you may order ANY COMBINATION of books in order to reach the desired discount rate. For example, in order to receive a 40% discount, you must order at least 20 copies, but to attain this number you can order any combination of books from our catalogue.

BOOK DISCOUNT RATE: (any combination)
Under 20 books: 35% DISCOUNT
20+ Books: 40% DISCOUNT
30+ Books: 50% DISCOUNT
50+ Books: 60% DISCOUNT
MAGAZINE DISCOUNT RATE: (any combination)
60< copies: 55% DISCOUNT
60> copies: 60% DISCOUNT

SHIPPING COSTS:
Books: Domestic- Will Bill
Books: Foreign- 12% of ORDER sent via M-BAG (surface shipping).
AIR SHIPPING IS MORE EXPENSIVE- CALL FOR QUOTE.
Magazines: Domestic- FREE shipping
Magazines: Foreign- 12% of ORDER sent via M-BAG (surface shipping) or sea route. AIR SHIPPING IS MORE EXPENSIVE- CALL FOR QUOTE.
 NOTE: M-BAGS REQUIRE A MINIMUM 15 POUND WEIGHT TO SHIP. IF YOUR ORDER IS TOO SMALL, YOU MAY NOT QUALIFY FOR THIS SPECIAL, LOW .79 CENT PER POUND SCALE. M-BAGS ARE NEVER INSURED AND ARE SENT AT DEALER'S RISK.

PAYMENT INFORMATION- For NEW Domestic customers, <u>payment must be submitted with your order</u>. Once you've made a few orders with us, you will be placed on a revolving 2-4 week credit line (depending on how often you order and how many copies you order). Late fees of 1½% per month (compounded) will be charged on orders not paid on time.   OVERSEAS dealers MUST ALWAYS pay in advance. Sorry about this, but you can thank your local unscrupulous book dealers for this. We have a collection agency, but it's difficult to collect moneys owed in Europe than it is here in the US. PAYMENT SHOULD BE MADE TO **"AXIS EUROPA".** Preferred Form: The best form is by Credit Card. We accept VISA/MC/Amex/Discover-Novus. Dealer's placing orders using credit cards will receive priority handling. Other Forms: International Postal Money Order, Bank Draft, or Cheque depositable in a US bank.

All orders are non-returnable, unless the book(s) have damage which occurred in production (such as a missing or blank page, spelling typos do not count). We will NOT replace a book that has been damaged in transit from your dealership to your customers!

ADVERTISING-

We have begun to accept advertising in our color journal ("Axis Europa") and in the back pages of the books which we produce. If you wish to find out more about how you can advertise in our journal and our books, please write into our editorial address and request ad rates. Hurry on this one! Our subscription list is approximately 1,600 dedicated and very specialized customers whose interest is German and Axis military history.

AXIS EUROPA MAGAZINE BACK ISSUES:
The following is a list of the major articles found in our journal. All back issues are low in quantity. Once an issue is sold out. It will only be available in Photocopy format, so please hurry and place your back issue orders now!

CURRENT SAMPLE ISSUE COST-
Domestic price: $8.00; Canadian price: $9.00, Overseas price: 10.00
SAVE MONEY!
SPECIAL SALE ORDER ALL BACK ISSUES
NOTE: SHIPPING IS ALREADY INCLUDED IN ALL BACK ISSUE ORDERS!

AXIS EUROPA ISSUES

ISSUE 1 - Serbian State & Frontier Guard (pt.1), Croatian Army in WWII (pt.1).

ISSUE 2 - Serbian State & Frontier Guard (pt.2), Croatian Army in WWII (pt.2), The Sword of Islam: The History of the 13.Waffen-Gebirgs- Division der-SS "Handschar" (pt.1).

ISSUE 3 - Croatian Army in WWII (pt.3), The Sword of Islam (pt.2), On the Cuff: The British Legion of St. George, Teutonic Magyars: Hungarian Volunteers of the Waffen-SS (pt.1).

ISSUE 4 - Croatian Army in WWII (pt.4), The Croatian Legion in Russia, Teutonic Magyars (pt.2), The Italian Decima X MAS in Russia, History of the Bosnian SS "Kama" Division, Croatian Troops Then & Now, Estonian Troops Then & Now.

ISSUE 5 - Croatian Army in WWII (pt.5), Teutonic Magyars (pt.3), For King & Fatherland: The History of the Montenegro Volunteer Corps (pt.1), German Police & Auxiliary Forces in Poland, 1939-1945 (pt.1), Serbian Troops Then & Now.

ISSUE 6 - Croatian Army in WWII (pt.6), Teutonic Magyars (pt.4), For King & Fatherland (pt.2), German Police & Auxiliary Forces in Poland, 1939-1945 (pt.2), Italian Elite: The Xth Decima MAS Division, 1943-1945 (pt.1).

ISSUE 7 - Croatian Army in WWII (pt.7), Teutonic Magyars (pt.5), For King & Fatherland (pt.3), German Police & Auxiliary Forces in Poland, 1939-1945 (pt.3), Italian Elite (pt.2), WWII Axis Military Postage Stamps, Slovenian Troops Then & Now.

ISSUE 8 - Croatian Army in WWII (pt.8), Teutonic Magyars (pt.6), For King & Fatherland (pt.4), Latvian Volunteers of the Waffen-SS & Order Police, 1941-1945.

ISSUE 9 - Croatian Army in WWII (pt.9), The Moslem Legion of the Sandjak, Albanian Collaborationist Forces 1943-44, New pictures of the Kaminski Brigade.

ISSUE 10 - Legion Stamp Propaganda: Axis Military Postage Stamps & Postcards, 1941-45, Uniforms & Insignia of the Croatian Air Force Legion, 1941-1945, Romania: A Brave Ally 1941-1944, Albanian Fascist Militia (revisited).

ISSUE 11 - The Carpathian (Ukrainian) Sic Units - 1939, The Arab Fascist Youth of Lybia, The Italian Expeditionary Corps in Russia 1941-42, German Police & Auxiliary Forces in Poland 1939-1945 (pt.4).

Military Truck. World War II Axis & Foreign Legion Medals and Badges. Croatian Navy in WWII, Book Reviews, plus much more!

ISSUE 16 - SPECIAL, LARGE, CHRISTMAS ISSUE (actually a book!). $17.95 + shipping. "CHETNIK: The Story of the Royal Yugoslav Army of the Homeland, 1941-1945." 64pp, many photos, maps, Orders of Battle, etc.! NOTE: THIS ISSUE/BOOK COSTS $17.95 (see book "15" in the list).

BACK ISSUE SALE-

Purchase Issues 1-15 for:
$118.00 DOMESTIC CUSTOMERS
$129.00 CANADIAN / MEXICAN CUSTOMERS
$139.00 OVERSEAS CUSTOMERS
Purchase Issues 1-15 & the Special (Book) Issue 16 at:
$130.00 DOMESTIC CUSTOMERS
$141.00 CANADIAN / MEXICAN CUSTOMERS
$151.00 OVERSEAS CUSTOMERS
Note: The Special "Book-15" Issue (No.16) Can only be purchased at this specially reduced price if you also order issues 1-15 of the journal. Otherwise, the "issue" will cost $17.95 plus shipping.

NOTE: If you're interested in being notified whenever a new book comes out in the German World War II Organizational Series (see pages 217-218), please drop us a line. Be sure to include your full name and address. If you wish to leave a "standing order" you must also supply us with your current credit card information (including expiration date).

GERMAN WORLD WAR II
ORGANIZATIONAL SERIES

by Dr. Leo G. Niehorster

Dr. Niehorster has produced a multi-volume work dealing with the complete organization of the German Wehrmacht (Armed Forces) in World War II.

Each oversized, perfect bound volume not only gives the reader the lengthy, German WWII Order of Battle , but also explains in text and schematic diagrams the organization of the German forces down to the minutest detail.

These volumes will become a valuable reference tool not only to military historians, and students of the war, but to game designers, wargamers, and even academics in military museums and universities. We will notify you of availability but do let us know that you're interested and you'll be placed on the mailing list.

Each perfect bound book is handsomely presented using a (German Army) Field Gray cover and sell for $22.00 + s&h

1/I	1939- Mechanized Army & SS units
1/II	1939- Army & SS units, HQ's, GHQ's
2/I	1940- Mechanized Army Divisions
2/II	1940- Mechanized GHQ & SS units
2/III	1940- Army & SS formations
2/III	1940- HQ's, GHQ & SS units
3/I	1941- Mechanized Army Divisions
3/II	1941- Mechanized GHQ & SS units
3/III	1941- Army & SS formations
3/III	1941- HQ's, GHQ & SS units
4/I	1942- Mechanized Army Divisions
4/II	1942- Mechanized GHQ & SS units
4/III	1942- Army & SS formations

4/IV	1942- HQ's, GHQ, & SS units
5/I	7/1943- Mechanized Army Divisions
5/II	7/1943- Mechanized GHQ & SS units
5/III	7/1943- Army & SS formations
5/IV	7/1943- HQ's, GHQ, & SS units
6/I	11/1943- Mechanized Army Divisions
6/II	11/1943- Mechanized GHQ & SS units
6/III	11/1943- Army & SS formations
6/IV	11/1943- HQ's, GHQ, & SS units
7/I	6/1944- Mechanized Army Divisions
7/II	6/1944- Mechanized GHQ & SS units
7/III	6/1944- Army & SS formations
7/IV	6/1944- HQ's, GHQ, & SS units
8/I	12/1944- Mechanized Army Divisions
8/II	12/1944- Mechanized GHQ & SS units
8/III-IV	12/1944- Army, SS ; HQ's, & GHQ, units
9/I	Luftwaffe Ground Combat Forces, 1942-45

AUTHORS-

AXIS EUROPA is constantly looking for authors who have articles or manuscripts dealing with the military history of the Axis forces in WWII. Your articles can be prepared on floppy disk (1.44 MB); Iomega zip drives (100 MB); While your book manuscripts can be sent via Iomega zip disk, or jazz disks (1.0 Gigabyte) . A "paper" copy of the ms/article must accompany the electronic copy. All submissions must be addressed to our business address: AXIS EUROPA BOOKS & MAGAZINES 53-20 207th Street, Bayside, N.Y. 11364   USA

NOTE: If you wish your manuscript or article returned, you must supply return postage and packaging. We are not responsible for uninsured parcels or letters.

SHIP CONTAINER COMPANIES
(For Overseas Dealers)

1] Clark World Wide Transportation Inc. / I.B.S.
   1307 Continental Drive,
   Abington, Maryland 21009 USA

2] Express Book Freight
   390 Campus Drive
   Somerset, New Jersey 08873 USA

The above two companies are reputable and while we make no claims as to reliability and liability, we can tell you that overseas companies use them on a regular basis. This leads us to think that they are reliable.

Overseas orders which are placed through any of the above ship container companies (or another, US based container company) will be given top priority.